CHRISTMAS IN ARCHANGEL

A memoir of life in the Merchant Navy 1939 - 1946

Ivan Hall.

Trafford
PUBLISHING

www.trafford.com

North America & international
toll-free: 1 888 232 4444 (USA & Canada)
phone: 250 383 6864 ♦ fax: 812 355 4082

DEDICATION

As will be apparent, these 'nautical memories' were written a few years ago solely for my family. I am told they may have a wider interest and so agree to them being published.

I do so in remembrance of Edna, who like thousands of other young women waited for her man, often not knowing where he was, when he would come back, or even if he would do so.

CONTENTS

Illustrations.

Illustrations.

Epilogue – The Atheltarn.

Maps

INTRODUCTION & ACKNOWLEDGEMENTS

One day as we sat in the dining room my daughter in law Joan was telling us about her father, the Army and Burma when she turned and said something to Adrian my son which I didn't catch, but his reply was "I don't know, he never tells us anything".

So here it is, or as much as I remember after sixty years or more. As I still have my Indentures and Discharge Book the names of ships and dates of voyages were available on to which to fit the memories. I also have my 'Sight Book' of the Atheltarn voyage—since it was then peace time it was not 'secret information'.

I'm just surprised that I've remembered so much but its only since I've been retired that I've had time to think about it. I have to say it's been quite nostalgic—after all, it was about all of my youth and where and when I grew from a boy to young manhood. It is not intended to be a history of the war at sea, or a critique of the way it was conducted. It is just what happened to me, and I was lucky, very!

Very rarely there is a word or phrase that one would not use in polite conversation, but remember, it was the Merchant Service I had joined, not the YMCA.

During the wartime period we knew little of what was happening beyond our visual horizon and often not much of what was happening within it, so I have referred to books to aid my memory and to fill in the background relating to that period. The following I found very useful.

- *The Fighting Admirals. British Admirals of the Second World War,* by Martin Stephen, 1991, United States Naval Inst.
- *Sea War 1939-45,* by Janusz Piekalkiewicz, 1987, Blandford Press.

- *The Atlantic Campaign. The Great Struggle at Sea 1939-1945,* by Dan van der Vat, *2001, Birlinn Ltd.*
- *Convoy! Drama in Arctic Waters,* by Paul Kemp, 2000, Brockhampton Press.
- *The South American Saint Line,* by P M Heaton, 1984, Gwent GB.
- *The Red Duster at War,* by J M Slader, 1988, W Kimber.
- *The Fourth Service. Merchantmen at War 1939-45,* by John Slader, 1997, Brick Tower Press.

I found the last book particularly useful although I object strongly to its title—we in the Merchant Marine were not fourth to anyone. The Navy, Army and Air Force were military services but we were civilians—at the outbreak of war all professional seamen. As the war progressed and manning became difficult, training schemes were set up to overcome the shortage and I believe that men called up for military service also had the option of joining, but civilians we were. Neither have I much liked the wartime name of Merchant Navy, which seems to imply a connection of some kind with the Royal Navy. We worked with the RN and were very grateful for their protection, but were fiercely independent of them. I prefer the title Merchant Marine, or more elegantly, Mercantile Marine. In peacetime the only thing we had in common with the RN was that we were both on ships that floated on water. We grew much closer together as the war progressed.

Rear Admiral Creighton, a Commodore, said of his merchant colleagues, "Ordinary unpretentious people, self contained, confident and calm. Their small talk generally nil, their speech usually abrupt, confined to the essentials and very much to the point. They uphold discipline by sheer character and personality for their powers of punishment under the Board of Trade Regulations are almost non-existent." I thank him for those words.

I hope it becomes apparent to the reader that I enjoyed my time at sea, I have had no regrets. The war changed things of course. Life became more hazardous and regulated but I was doing something I liked, something I thought I was good at, certainly something useful, and I survived. If I had not gone to sea when I did goodness knows what would have happened to me. You will know of course that I do not claim these experiences to be in any way unique—there were thousands of us, all in the same boat, or perhaps I should say convoys.

Finally, I wish to thank my elder son Laurence, who has patiently and diligently spent much time bringing to order my rambling reminiscences and making them into a readable narrative.

Ivan Hall

November 2007.

Photographs are the property of the author except for those attributed to the Imperial War Museum.

1

THE ESCAPE

A Black Country Boyhood

There is a saying that it's better to be born lucky than rich. It would have made life a little easier to have been born a little richer but on the whole I'm content to have been born lucky. This is perhaps not obvious to others and it's a conclusion I've reached only in old age— since I've had time to think about it!

The first real stroke of luck came in the August of 1938 when I was sixteen years old. Having left Darlaston Intermediate School, our selective central school in that part of the industrial Midlands, at fourteen years of age as so many of us did, I had been working at Samuel Platt & Sons Ltd., a Wednesbury engineering firm making rather old fashioned machine tools, for a little over two years. Not one of my friends or acquaintances gave a thought to or was interested in academic education and neither were our parents. Father was suspicious and distrustful of academics. His Christian faith and indeed his life were based on the Bible and he thought that many of them were publishing opinions that were inimical to and incompatible with his faith.

One must remember too that Darlaston was then a manufacturing town of the 'Black Country' and predominantly working class—in the widest sense. The opinion of most people would have been that schools were to teach children to read, write and calculate but not much else mattered. Brought up in that environment we children thought more or less the same although I would probably have added science and woodwork which I thought were useful and music and games because I liked them. Our ambition was to leave school as early as possible and to start work in a career with prospects such as a skilled trade and to obtain national qualifications— the 'great depression' when thousands were 'on the dole' was not far back—but by then I was no longer happy.

My job was not at all challenging mentally and I could quite easily cope with the craft side of things. In other words it was getting boring. There was much petty jealousy in the workshop and I felt that a little of it was directed my way. If I felt that at sixteen years what would it be like for life? In addition to the weekday work hours of 8 a.m. to 5.30 p.m. and 8 a.m. to 12.30 p.m. on Saturdays, my work friend and myself attended night classes at the County Technical College three nights a week with homework to do at weekends as well—but for what? Perhaps to become Pattern Shop Foreman and exceptionally, one of the managers. From what I could see of them that was not an attractive prospect.

I was also becoming increasingly worried about life at home. My devout parents belonged to a group or sect known to themselves as the 'Brethren'. Father always seemed to wish to deny that they were Plymouth Brethren though I'm unaware of what difference there was. It seemed to me that their belief was that life in this wicked world was only a prelude to eternity in Heaven or Hell and was more to be endured than enjoyed. They had the conviction that theirs was the only true way to eternal life in Heaven. I suppose today one would call them 'fundamentalists'. The Bible was accepted as the literal truth. I was not convinced. I never had been, and as I got older I became more doubtful. I had not become an atheist but I was certainly agnostic. This I could not tell my parents, I think it would have broken their hearts. I was their only child, they were good parents and I could not do that to them.

What could I do? The only traditional ways for a working class boy to leave home in those days were to join the Forces or the Police. Father, who had been imprisoned in the First World War for being an uncompromising conscientious objector had made it clear to me over the years that on no account would he allow me to join anything of a military nature. I was not even allowed to join the Boy Scouts and his opinion of the Police was scathing.

The future looked bleak, but then came the luck. There was in the August of 1938, in Glasgow, an exhibition the theme of which was 'The British Empire' (we had one in those days) and someone in the firm organised a works outing to see it. I said I would like to go and father said he would go too. A 'special' train was used and from what I remember of the size of the group I think it likely that more than just our firm was involved.

Except for one item I remember nothing of the exhibition at all, but since it was about the Empire it was probably concerned with Britain's position as a trading nation with the colonies and dominions. Since all overseas trade was carried in merchant shipping in those days it followed that there was a stand about life in the Merchant Service. So there it was—the possible escape. It didn't hit me like the revelation of St. Paul; rather it dawned slowly but surely.

It all turned out to be surprisingly easy. I first put the suggestion to Mother who said she would speak to Father. It might not have been too much of a surprise to them for they would know that I had always been interested in ships and the sea. As a small boy I never wanted to go to any other place than New Brighton for the summer holidays. Crossing the Mersey on the ferry was always tremendously exciting. At New Brighton I could sail my boat on the yachting pool. From the sands one could watch the liners and freighters arriving and leaving the Liverpool docks across the river, when the tide was out one could walk around the lighthouse, and most fascinating of all one could travel on the Liverpool Overhead Railway the whole length of the docks, see what was going on and perhaps stop off for a tour of one of the ocean liners.

Perhaps I had always wanted to go to sea but thought it impossible until the Glasgow exhibition showed the way. Even now, over seventy years later, I can still remember most of a poem I 'learned by heart' at the junior school. I don't remember the title and the poet's name but here is what I do.

> Once upon a time there was a schoolboy
> Who lived in a cottage by the sea,
> And the very first thing he could remember
> Was the rigging of the schooners by the key.
>
> He could watch them when he woke from his window
> With the tall cranes hoisting out the freight,
> And he used to think of shipping as a sea cook
> And sailing to the Golden Gate.
>
> There were brigantines with timber out of Norway
> Oozing with the syrups of pine,
> And rusty dusty schooners out of Sunderland,
> And ships of the Blue Cross line.
>
> He used to buy those yellow penny dreadfuls
> And read them as he fished for conger eels,
> And listen to the lapping of the water,
> The green and oily water round the keels.
>
> To tumble down a hatch into a cabin
> Was better than the best of broken rules,
> For the smell of 'em was like a Christmas dinner
> And the feel of 'em was like a box of tools.
>
> He is perched upon a high stool in London
> And the Golden Gate is very far away,
> They caught him and they caged him like a squirrel,
> He is totting up accounts and going grey.
>
> But before he goes to sleep in the evenings
> The very last thing that he can see
> Is the sailor boys a dancing in the moonlight

By the capstan that stands upon the quay,
To the tune of an old concertina
By the capstan that stands upon the quay.

There are other poems which I learned later—'Dirty British coaster with a salt caked smoke stack, butting through the channel in the mad March days', 'Sea Fever', 'Drake is in his hammock and a thousand miles away' and of course 'The Ancient Mariner'. The first was my favourite.

There was also a Children's Hour serial programme on Thursday radio at five fifteen which I unfailingly rushed home from school to listen to called 'Java Ho!' It was about the adventures of a young boy on a sailing ship out there.

Sometime later, having discussed it with Mother, Father told me that they had thought and prayed about it and had come to the conclusion that if that was what I wanted, and he pointed out that what one wanted in one's youth could change as one got older, then they would agree. He knew someone in Cardiff who worked in the office of a shipping company and he would write to them for advice.

Just after Christmas 1938 arrangements had been made for me to become an apprentice to the B & S Shipping Company of Cardiff to become a deck officer. I was to find out that all their ships were named Saint something or other and the Company was known to seamen as the Saint Line. The saintly names seemed to have nothing to do with religion or Christianity.

Early in January 1939 on a freezing cold day with no heating in the railway carriage, I went with my father to the offices of the Shipping Federation in Liverpool where the signing of the Indentures took place. I remember that first there was a medical examination and eyesight test of which the test for colour vision was an important part—the ability to recognise and differentiate between small spots of red, green and white light in a darkened room simulating the navigation lights of ships at sea. These tests would be repeated later at the Certificate of Competency examinations. Afterwards, having signed on the dotted line (I still have the indentures) it was off to the outfitting department of the Liverpool Sailors' Home to be measured for the uniform and complete sea outfit.

Whilst there the man who was measuring me asked what shipping company I was joining. When I told him he said, "I think they are on the Plate run aren't they?" I had to say I didn't know—really I didn't understand what he meant. It was not until we were on the way to South America that I discovered that Buenos Aries was on the River Plate.

I still have the receipt from the Sailors' Home including a list of the items of clothing supplied. The cost was something over twenty pounds, delivered—seems awfully cheap these days but would probably have represented four to five weeks wages for my father. The quality of the number one uniform was superb—I was still wearing the trousers when I was torpedoed four years later, which also shows that either I was a big lad at sixteen or I had not put much weight on since. It was quite an event when the railway man dropped off my first sea-bag at home in Sandwell Avenue.

Once this 'enrolling' was completed I gave notice to leave the firm for which I was working. I had by this time quite a collection of woodworking tools and I was able to sell most of them to 'Young Harry' who had followed me first into the Works Office and later to the Pattern Shop. I passed to Father the money I received to help with the cost of fitting out.

It was a great surprise to everyone. To people living in the Black Country, going to sea meant joining the Navy. Although they knew the Merchant Service existed, it was not something to which they gave a second thought unless there was some maritime disaster and then they thought only of passenger liners. I could sense there was a feeling of envy too and some of the older men said so and wished that they had got away when younger.

Then came the letter telling me to join the SS St. Merriel lying in Millwall Docks at London. There seems to be a bit of confusion here in that the date of my signing the Indentures is given as the twelfth of January 1939 but my record of joining the St. Merriel shows the fourteenth, an impossibly short space of time.

Father went with me travelling by train to London and by taxi to the docks—a few words to the policeman at the gate and we were soon alongside the ship. By this time it was mid-afternoon. We climbed up the accommodation ladder, someone explained to us that the 'Mate' was not aboard—he was due back from leave in a few days—but we were shown to my cabin. A quick look around, Father said goodbye and took his leave. That was it! I had escaped! I knew what I had escaped from, but not what I had escaped to.

2

THE SHIPS AND THE MEN

Life in the pre-war Merchant Service

In those days the ports and docks were full of shipping of all shapes and sizes from all over the world—but most of it was British. At the small end of the range were the coasters, which did just that, carrying freight from one local port to another. Some of them were quite small—both ships and ports. Their masters were not noted for their skills at celestial navigation and were reputed to find their way around by their sense of smell and the colour of the water. There was some truth in this! Carriage by water, whether sea, river or canal was the cheapest form of transport and there was not the desperate rush that we have today.

Next came the slightly larger boats which traded over the North Sea to the Baltic, Scandinavia and north European ports with others going down Channel to the Biscay ports, Spain, Portugal and perhaps into the Mediterranean. Many of these were on regular scheduled runs. It was the ship owner's ambition to get his ship out of port on Friday and sailing to its destination over the weekend so that it could start discharging and loading on the Monday, ready for a next Friday sailing. These were known as 'the weekly boats', noted for hard work and small pay, but coming back to the home port every week or two. Although the normal working day was eight hours, on this type of ship it was ten hours on days of departure or arrival and also for most of the time at sea.

Larger again were the 'deep-sea' boats and tankers. Amongst the former were the ocean going freighters—'tramps'—which would carry almost anything from anywhere to anywhere else in the world. Some belonged to small companies owning perhaps two or three ships, others to companies owning perhaps a hundred or more. One company may have bought their ships on the second hand market; others would have them built to their own recognisable design and always by the same builders. Such ships were instantly recognisable by their silhouette and such a firm that comes to mind was Andrew Weir of the Clyde whose ship names always ended in 'bank'. They were often away from the UK for two years or more and were so well founded that during the war some of them were converted to Ack Ack Cruisers. Many companies had nicknames—not all of them affectionate—'Ropner's Navy', 'Hungry Hains', 'Tatems with a 'T' on the funnel but none on the table', and so on.

Other companies plied a regular trade. The United Africa Co. plied to the African west coast, The New Zealand Shipping Co. is self-evident and the B & S Shipping Co. sailed to South America. The regular traders frequently had a limited amount of passenger accommodation since a ship could carry up to twelve passengers without having to carry a doctor and the newer ships of the B & S Company were in this category.

Then of course there were the liners, whose main role was to carry passengers but incidentally took some freight and often mail. These included the Royal Mail Steamship Co. and the Blue Star Line which both traded to South America. Finally there were ships designed for special purposes –such as tankers, whalers, refrigerated cargo ships, banana boats, cable layers, Trinity House ships, tugs, salvage ships and thousands of fishing boats, all manned by men of the Merchant Service, who themselves were of many nationalities.

Perhaps in view of what soon happened I should mention the RNR or Royal Naval Reserve. Some merchant seamen, at all levels, were volunteer members and received periodic training in the RN so that there was a reserve of officers and men available should they be required. Some shipping companies encouraged their employees to join.

It has perhaps become apparent by now that the largest unit of organisation in the Merchant Service was the company fleet with their Marine Superintendent at its head, the smaller units being the ships of which the B & S Company had at that time I think about ten. There was no towering hierarchy as in the Armed Services.

At the appropriate time the Ship's Articles (which could be described as a contract of service) were opened at the port Shipping Office and the crew was signed on. If I remember correctly the period of service was for two years or the ship's return to the UK if earlier. Generally, officers, maybe petty officers and some crew would be 'company's men', i.e. they would stay employed with that company and hope to earn promotion within it, as in civilian employment—which of course it was. Others would prefer to be more footloose and when the voyage ended take their Discharge Book and pay off money and clear off. If and when they needed to earn more money they would go to a Shipping Office and find out what ships were signing on and if there were any jobs available. It was this freedom which was attractive to youngsters with no responsibilities.

Not so the apprentices, in some companies called cadets. They were indeed company's men, bound by a legal document for four years and they did what they were told.

3

THE NEW BOY AND HIS FIRST SHIP

The St. Merriel sails for Antwerp

The first ships owned by the B & S Line were old ones, which were bought in the mid 1930's. I understand that a government scheme then existed to encourage the building of new ships, under which a company that scrapped some old ships would receive funding to have a new one built. However the St. Merriel which I joined was not one of those.

Built in 1925, she was old fashioned but not bad looking, strongly built and comfortable in a seaway. She was a flush shelter decked ship of almost 5,000 tons net, something over 450ft long, about 50ft in the beam and I think the loaded draft was 26ft. plus. Built on the N.E. coast as a coal burner she had at sometime been converted to oil burning (thank goodness). The full crew was the Captain and three Deck Officers, four Engineers, one Radio Operator, a Chief Steward, Cook, Messroom Steward, Galley Boy, Cabin Boy, Boatswain, Carpenter, eight AB Seamen, one Ordinary Seaman, three Donkeymen greasers, three Firemen, and of course the two Apprentices, a total of thirty three.

The seamen lived in a triangular shaped room on the port side of the forecastle, the firemen and donkeymen to starboard. In the bridge block, immediately in front of number three hold, the Captain's accommodation was on the starboard side of the boat deck with the Sparks and WT cabin on the port side. Above was the chartroom and bridge. Below at main deck level was the Officer's saloon plus the pantry, with their accommodation to port and the Chief Steward and two empty cabins (one of them labelled Hospital) to starboard. Abaft number three hatch was the galley followed by Engineers' accommodation to port and to starboard their mess-room and cabins for Bosun and Chippy, catering staff and two cabins for four Apprentices—since there were only two of us we had one each.

Propelled by a triple expansion reciprocating steam engine with three Scotch boilers, the power plant of many ocean freighters of her vintage, a good days run would be 240 sea miles. The engine room trunking ran up between our cabins on one side and the engineers' quarters on the other, and the THUMP thump thump, THUMP thump thump of the engine 'big ends' would be a familiar sound for weeks on end, so much so that when it stopped the silence was uncomfortable.

What happened during the rest of that first day I don't remember as things were somewhat confused and memory fades. I've come to the conclusion that the ship had completed discharging and that repairs and maintenance were taking place. A cargo ship in port is an untidy object with derricks hoisted and swung at all angles, hatch beams and covers lying on the deck, wires and ropes all over the place. There was not much of a crew on board and whatever work was necessary was being done by riggers—longshoremen paid by the day. I must have drawn an issue of bed linen at sometime for I remember being impressed that I had a Dunlopillow mattress to sleep on. The cabin was about eight feet by six feet six inches, with two bunks one above the other. I didn't know then but I was to be its sole occupant for the next twelve months.

Late in the afternoon the Boatswain turned up at my cabin door. A genial barrel chested individual in his late thirties with the soft Scots accent of the Hebrides, he was from Stornoway and named McLeod. I never knew his Christian name; Boatswains were always known and addressed as 'Bose'. He had been on leave and had just returned to be told to keep me occupied until the Mate returned. I had no idea who the Mate was but it eventually became clear to me that he was the Chief Officer, as far as I was concerned the Big Boss. The ranks of Officer and Captain were really courtesy titles since the Captain signed on as 'Master' and the Deck Officers as 'Mates'. The Bosun said that tomorrow morning I should turn out in my working dungarees. My meals were to be taken at second sitting in the Engineers' Mess Room which was at the forward end of our cabin corridor or alleyway.

The next morning the Steward called me in to breakfast and on that occasion I was the only one at second sitting. He offered corn flakes or porridge (often called 'burgoo' and made from oatmeal) which I thought was a reasonable start, then followed curry and rice. I doubt if I had heard of this before, never mind eaten it, but told that it was a standard breakfast dish on this ship I thought I had better get used to it. This was followed by bacon and egg, toast and marmalade, tea or coffee. I thought at the time that if this was a sample I was not going to starve. So it proved. Though not Cordon Bleu the meals were always substantial and the quality really depended upon the skill of the cook at that time. Every deep-sea ship had to have a Board of Trade certificated cook, though their expertise and enthusiasm varied. The one drawback with the St. Merriel was that she had no refrigerator, only an ice box, and for how long we had fresh food depended upon the skill with which it was packed by the Steward and Cook.

The Bosun collected me after breakfast, pointing out that normally the working day began an hour before breakfast at 7 am. but as it was my first day and the Mate was not yet aboard he'd let me lie in. He then took me on to the lower bridge, unlaced and removed a canvas cover to reveal a green verdigris encrusted piece of brass machinery, which I learned, was the reserve or stand-by engine room telegraph. The one in general use was on the bridge above. I was provided with a can containing some kind of oil, a piece of bath brick, an old broken bladed kitchen knife and an assortment of rags, pieces of canvas and cotton waste and was told to clean it.

Assuring me that he would be back later I was left to it. What a job! The thing could not have been cleaned for years and for the following two and three quarter years I was on that ship it would not be cleaned again. With hindsight it was a very good way of testing my 'stickability' and getting me out of the way for the day. I have never liked brass cleaning since.

Later in the day the other apprentice named Barley turned up. From what I remember he had been with the ship for about twelve months and had been home on leave. He was friendly enough and said it was our responsibility when in port to hoist the Ensign on the sternpost and the House Flag on the main mast at eight o'clock in the morning and to take them down at sunset. He then showed me how to make the hitches. Next morning he said a telegram had arrived to say that his mother (or some other near relative) was dangerously ill and would the Captain send him home. With that he disappeared, leaving me to do the flags!

He did not return but later I heard the true story from him. During the previous voyage he had written home complaining of being bullied by the Mate and his father in turn had written to the Company. When Barley went on leave he thought the Mate was to be transferred to another ship but when he returned and discovered that the Mate was returning too, and undoubtedly would be after his blood, he had telephoned his father to send the phoney telegram.

Later on when the Mate got to know me I heard his side of things and I actually got on quite well with him. A Welshman with the unlikely name of Campbell he was renowned for having a short temper. He expected his orders to be carried out forthwith and to his satisfaction, and if they were, all was well. He had after all a very responsible job and apart from the engine room and the catering to look after it was he who ran the ship and was entitled not to suffer fools gladly.

Over the next few days the crew returned. Quite a number were from the Bosun's home town, including a younger brother named Donald whose body size was even more impressive. They were a grand lot as I was to find out, for although as apprentices we were destined, if we made the grade, to become officers or mates, we were to 'pull and haul with the men' as one historical figure put it. Perhaps even more so, for whilst the hours of the men were regulated by the Merchant Shipping Act and extra work was 'overtime', as Company's men we were always available for nothing. The engine room firemen and donkeymen were Maltese—whether this was the policy of the Company or the Chief Engineer I don't know. Later, when I served on a ship which had Liverpool firemen I could see the point as the Maltese were a cheerful and affable lot.

Another apprentice arrived in place of the disappeared Barley. He was newer than I was, and as I had then been on board for five or six days, by that margin I was Senior Apprentice on my first trip! Named Paul he was from South Wales, about my age and size but a little heavier and perhaps a little older. He was a rugby player, dark complexioned with black curly hair. He had charm and fancied himself with the ladies and was certainly more worldly-wise than I at that time. I think he came straight from school, he had certainly never worked and did not at all take to the dirty physical jobs we had to do at times which did not endear him to the Mate. Paul didn't talk much of why he was at sea and certainly he made no secret that he would rather be at home with his girl friend. I wondered whether his parents disapproved and had engineered his removal.

Also on board at this time were some officers' wives and when we sailed across to Antwerp some of them came with us which was one of the perks of working for the Saint Line I suppose. I remember with any clarity only one of them and she was the wife of the First Mate or Chief Officer. This must be because she was a blonde with an attractive, friendly and lively personality with a ready smile for us boys.

We sailed in the dark of one late January evening. We had to wait until then for the slack water at high tide when the dock gates were opened. All day we had been battening down hatches, lowering derricks and tidying away the gear. We had hoisted the Blue Peter flag to show that we were to sail, and when the Pilot was aboard we showed a white all round light over a red one. At 'Stand by fore and aft' when the deck crew went to their allotted stations for entering and leaving port, my place as Senior Apprentice was on the forecastle head with the Mate, Chippy and half of the sailors. Paul's place was aft with the Second Mate, Bosun and the rest of the seamen.

Tugs were made fast, it was 'Let go fore and aft' and we were soon through the lock gates and into the busy Thames. Nearing midnight as we were heading out towards the North Sea on passage for Antwerp, we were stood down and told what watches we were in. As Senior Apprentice I was on the 'four to eight' and told to get off to bed, as I had to be on watch at four in the morning! Paul, on the 'eight to twelve' could look forward very soon to a good night's sleep

All merchant ships at that time when at sea worked a three watch system, sometimes known as four (hours) on and eight off, which meant that one was always on watch at the same time of day. Traditionally the Mate took the 'four to eight' which left him free during the day to do his office work, supervise the daily work of the ship, perhaps have a nap during the early afternoon and get a reasonable nights sleep before his early morning watch. If the weather was favourable and it fitted into his watch times he usually 'made a fix' by star sights at dawn and dusk when it was possible to see both stars and the horizon at the same time.

The Second Mate had the role of 'navigator' and took the 'graveyard' watch of midnight to four a.m. and midday to four p.m. This enabled him to take the morning sights immediately after breakfast, work them up ready for fixing the noon position and any other routine work connected with the navigation which was his responsibility under the Captain. He also had one other simple but essential duty and that was to wind the chronometer every morning at nine o'clock—without accurate time we couldn't find longitude—but we were at that time blessed with a GMT radio signal.

That left the Third Mate to do the 'eight to twelve' which was certainly the most congenial as far as normal sleeping was concerned. This was intentional. For most Third Officers this was their first experience of watchkeeping responsibility and the Captain, always known on board as 'the Old Man', would naturally want to keep an eye on him. Thus to some extent the Third Mate's watch was also the Old Man's watch, and naturally he had the best! He also took part in the daily noon sights ceremony, was responsible for maintaining the efficiency of the lifeboats and life saving equipment, had to ensure that the steering gear and all the bridge communications were functioning when preparing to sail and was generally the Old Man's dogsbody. On arrival and departure his place was on the bridge assisting the master and pilot and keeping a record. In port all mates took part in supervising the discharge or loading and stowage of cargo under the supervision of the First Mate, as usually did the apprentices too.

Ships engineers had to have served an apprenticeship with a marine engineering firm before applying to a shipping company for employment. Having gained sufficient experience of seatime watch keeping as a junior engineer—on our class of ship they would be Fourth or Third Engineers—they could then sit for their Second Engineers Certificate (Motor or Steam), and with further experience their 'Chief's'. Ambitious types could do 'Extra Chief's'.

To revert to the watch system. There were two ABs and an apprentice on two of the watches and two ABs and the ordinary seaman on the third. That left two ABs over, who were put on daywork and usually they were a couple of older more experienced seamen who could be trusted to do a good job. The Mate in consultation with the Bosun decided all this. The watches themselves were divided into periods of steering, stand by and look out. To be on 'stand by' meant that one kept an ear open for any summoning whistle from the officer of the watch and reported to the bridge. It might mean turning the hold ventilators to suit a new direction of the wind, it might be to read the log or it may simply mean that the Mate on watch needed a brew of tea. Two other essential duties were to keep the galley fires going and at the appropriate time call the next watch, make them tea and make sure they were up and ready.

On the 'four to eight' morning watch it was a bit more complicated. The galley boy was called at a quarter to six—he called the cook; the mess boys and stewards were called at six thirty; the boatswain, chippy and day men immediately afterwards and a can of tea brewed for the latter. The next watch of seamen was called just after seven so that they could have 'a seven bells breakfast' before going on watch. One didn't have to rouse the Third Mate, by then the stewards were at work and he was awakened by them with a cup of tea before going on watch and relieved at eight thirty for his breakfast by the Second Mate.

Obviously it was necessary to know where everyone slept as it was a terrible crime to wake the wrong person. One became aware of differing sleeping habits. Some only needed a light touch and were instantly awake, others slept so soundly that one had to almost shake them out of their bunk or they would immediately go to sleep again.

Life at sea was regulated by the Bells. The controlling one on the bridge was struck at the appropriate time by the helmsman and during the hours of darkness was repeated by the lookout on the forecastle head. Eight Bells, struck in four pairs of two, was struck every four hours when the watch changed. One hour into the watch was Two Bells, two hours in was Four Bells and three hours in was Six Bells. There were also additional bells.

Having seemingly just gone off to sleep I had a rude awakening to be told by the standby man that it was a quarter to four in the morning, it had just gone One Bell and I was due to go on watch in a quarter of an hour. He said it would be cold and a bit rough and it was. Neither Paul nor I was as yet able to steer and so our watches consisted of an hour stand by, two hours lookout and a further hour of stand by, leaving the ABs to do the steering.

I rigged myself out in what warm gear I had—oilskins, seaboots, jerseys and an Astrakhan lined hat with earflaps. Nothing happened during my stand by and at Two Bells or five o'clock I went up to the forecastle head to relieve the lookout, who it turned out was the Bosun's brother. I must say that I met with nothing but kindness from all the seamen. They knew we were first trip apprentices and had it all to learn and if we were prepared to get stuck in they would respond and be helpful. He explained to me the procedure, which was that if one saw a light on the starboard side one struck once on the forecastle head bell. A light on the port side was two strokes and if there appeared a light right ahead one struck three times. When I heard the hourly bells struck on the bridge I was to repeat them. At Six Bells when I was relieved I should look to see that the mast-head lights and the port and starboard sidelights were on and if all was well shout to the officer of the watch on the bridge 'Lights are bright sir'. I was a bit suspicious that this was a leg-pull but it was true enough.

I don't think there could have been a more testing introduction to a life on the ocean wave than those two hours. It was not really the ocean of course but the North Sea which, being shallower, has shorter and choppier waves. Being a light ship we pitched and bounced all over the place. One moment as the bows came up one's weight was thrust violently and irremovably into one's seaboots, only for the bows to go crashing down again leaving one almost airborne and weightless and at the same time rolling from side to side. I was not sick, but for a while I was feeling very ropy. By the end of the stint I didn't feel too bad but I was very cold. I was able to eat my breakfast.

I remember nothing about the rest of the day until the early hours of darkness when we moored alongside what appeared to be a timber built pierhead that I was told was Flushing in Holland on the north side of the River Scheldt. There we stayed for a short while whilst we bunkered, then it was up river some miles to Antwerp. It's my recollection that during this last part of the passage the crew had to 'stand by fore and aft', I suppose for safety reasons, with the Mate on the foc'stle head and Chippy standing by the anchor windlass.

What I clearly remember is the tiredness and the cold wind. Some of the seamen and myself sheltered from the latter behind the 'break' of the foc'stle head. The steam pipes to the anchor windlass ran along the main deck, vertically up the break and on to the windlass. They were protected with a flat steel guard and there was a bit of warmth in this shield. Whilst the seamen seemed unconcerned by the elements and chattered on in lively fashion I propped myself up against the guard to get what heat I could and slowly dozed off on my feet.

I remember little of Antwerp. To a lad of sixteen it was merely a somewhat strange city, and with no money to spend it was of little interest. Within sight of our mooring was a tramway system which went into the city—not the old grinding two deckers which were still running in some British cities, but single deckers towing a second coach and which seemed to go at a terrific speed, honking their Wild West horns as they belted down the central reservation. (Why all this fuss now about the Midland Metro? Such systems existed all over the world pre-war and some countries had the good sense to keep them).

The dockers were Flemings and spoke Flemish of course, which was beyond my ken. They looked so neat and tidy in their washed denims whereas our dockers seemed to dress entirely in old clothes. But the noise! They seemed to be forever shouting and gesticulating in rage at each other as though they were about to erupt into violence. They were not of course, it was just that I was not used to their manner.

As well as loading by crane from the quay side we also had motorised barges moored along the offside from which we loaded with our own derricks. Some of these barges were half the length of our ship and had families living aboard. They were always spotlessly clean.

A lot of the cargo we loaded was steel in various forms: rods and wire for reinforcing concrete, some of it made up into mesh, rails for railway track, together with manufactured goods in crates and boxes and cement in paper sacks. There were five hatches and holds with 'tween decks but there was no transverse bulkhead between number four and five holds which meant this was one huge long cavern, ideal for long lengths of rail track. These were slung by the stevedores, two or three at a time, in chain slings so that they hung just off the vertical and were lowered into number four hold. Other men would lasso the bottom end with a steel wire and with the steam winch haul it aft into the number five hold as the sling was lowered.

Slowly a platform of steel rails was built up. I was always relieved when the first two or three layers were in since I dreaded a rail slipping out of the sling and going through the ship's bottom but it never happened. Although this long hold was a great convenience it worried me later in wartime as a torpedo smashing into that large void would have been a disaster. Fortunately that didn't happen either. To prevent the ship becoming too stiff or bottom heavy with the weight of the steelwork some of the bagged cement was loaded into the 'tween decks.

All would be discharged later in South American ports starting in the north of Brazil and working down to the Argentine. It was the Mate's responsibility to see that the cargo was loaded in such a way that the correct cargo for any port was accessible at that time.

It was only later that I realised I was a witness to Britain's decline as a trading nation. It was a boast that the Argentine railway system had been built by the British, yet there we were taking out German materials (for that was where the barges were coming from) for their maintenance.

In the last week of January the crew was paid off and a new crew was signed on. Being inexperienced, I was unaware that because so many of the crew signed on again for 'another trip' this was an indication of a contented crew, and so it proved.

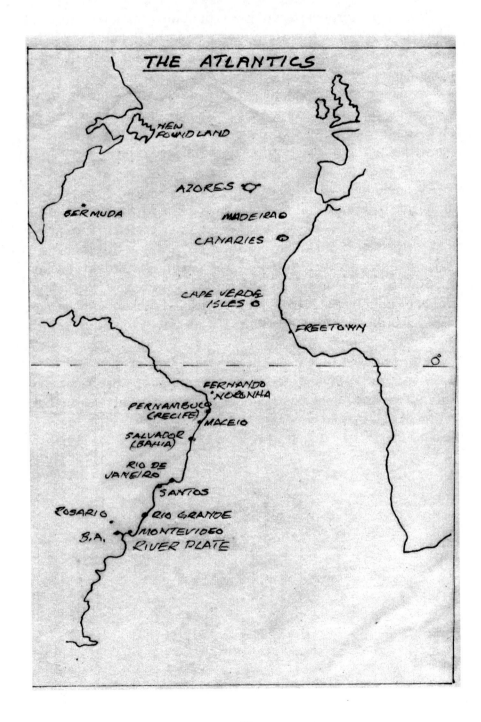

4

FIRST VOYAGE TO SOUTH AMERICA

Learning the ropes on board the St. Merriel

We left Antwerp during the early days of February 1939 and immediately began preparing for the long voyage south.

Derricks were lowered into their crutches and lashed down,
their rigging and gear was removed and lowered into the nearest
hold space and hatches were securely battened down with a good
heavy tarpaulin on top. Chippy went around the hatches with a sack
of new wedges and made sure all was tight. Mooring ropes were
stowed away in the fore and after peaks. In short, everything that
was moveable was stowed below. Chippy put steel bars through the
anchor cables above the hawse pipes so that they could not accidentally run out. Where the cables passed below deck down the spurl-
ing pipes, he packed them around with hessian and slapped cement
on top so that in the event of us 'taking them over green' the water
could not disappear down into the chain locker.

Next, it was down to the Engine Room to ask for 'water on deck'.
Out came the hoses and the great wash and scrub down began. We
all tackled this with enthusiasm. Sailors like a clean ship and we
all felt a lot better after the detritus of being in port was washed
away. From now on, unless the weather was extremely bad, every
day began at seven o'clock with a complete wash down of the ship

and when we reached the tropics we could do it in traditional bare footed style!

In addition to the watch keeping hours all the seamen and we apprentices had to do two hours deck work on four days of the week, which were known strangely as 'field days'. For those of us on the 'four to eight' watch our hours were from nine to eleven a.m. Monday to Thursday. Those days entering and leaving port were also ten hour days.

In a few days time we were breaking out of the Channel Approaches to head south across The Bay. It was still cold but in the South Westerlies the wind had lost that freezing bite that it had around the River Scheldt.

Attention was now given to the paintwork and varnished wood-work; it all had to be washed clean, or as the seamen called it, 'soogied'. I never did find out the origin of the word. Prepared by the Bosun, the cleaning element was a handful of soda and per-haps a nugget of soft soap dissolved in a bucket of warm water. We worked in teams of two. The first man with the soogie and cloth loosening the dirt, while the second man followed on with a bucket or two of fresh water, washing off and then drying—except it was not as straightforward as that—the St. Merriel, as other ships of her age, was riveted together and it needed some dextrous cloth work at times to work around the rivet heads, especially in the corners.

The soda could have an adverse effect upon delicate hands and I usually got a crack or two which would sting like the dickens. It didn't much bother the horny handed sailors. Paul was always be-moaning the state of his hands. The worst soda was some proprie-tary brand of cleaning agent, which the Bosun referred to as 'caustic', and which made one's nails soft and turned them brown.

During one early morning watch with the weather a bit rough and spray coming over the foc'stle head I was keeping lookout on the starboard wing of the bridge when the Mate walked across from his side and questioned me. Where did I live? Had any of my for-bears or relations been to sea? Why then had I decided to go to sea? Probably with thoughts of his wife still in his mind he said "You're a bloody fool!" End of conversation.

After just over a week we were all clean, tidy and ship shape. Days were longer and brighter, the weather was getting warmer and it was not such a bind getting up at four in the morning because the dawn was not far away.

The Mate determined to teach me to steer. I remember the lesson very well and found it not difficult. I remember him saying that if you ride a bike and turn the bars to the left the front wheel turns, the bike follows and when you've turned enough you straighten the bars and the bike goes straight on. It's not like that with a ship. The turning centre is about one third of the way from forrard, about where the bridge is. When you turn the wheel to port there is a pause while the water pressure builds up on the rudder and the ship's head then begins to turn to port but the two thirds of the ship behind the bridge swings out to starboard. To settle on a new course it is necessary to 'ease off the helm' or straighten the rudder before getting to the new course and then to apply counter rudder to stop the ship from swinging too far.

The essential of being a good helmsman is anticipation. The ship is continually under the influence of wind and waves and knowing or feeling what is going to happen and applying helm to correct it in good time before it does occur is the essential art. There is some truth in the saying that a good helmsman steers with his feet—that is, he can feel and sense what the ship is going to do and apply the necessary helm in time to keep the ship on it's course. With the old magnetic compasses which swung from side to side with each roll of the ship it was indeed an art. Paul and I soon acquired the skill and our watchmates were as pleased as we were for the watches could now take up their proper rhythm.

Every Sunday morning at sea was the 'Old Man's Inspection' when, resplendent in full uniform and supported by the Mate and Chief Steward he made his tour of the ship. There was no 'bull' but one had to be neatly turned out, the cabin clean neat and tidy, the brasswork of gimballed paraffin lamp, drawer pulls and porthole polished. That first Sunday morning was the first time Captain Owens had spoken to me or I to him. He was a sturdily built Welshman, in his mid forties I suppose, with an air of quiet confidence acquired by long experience. I was to find him a kind and fatherly figure who later on was to respond to my enthusiasm and good examination results with interest and encouragement.

I have written of the Old Man and the Mate but what of the other Deck Officers? The Second Mate we hardly saw since neither of us was on his watch. Paul saw more of him than I did because he was in his after guard. He was reputed to have served his sea time for the Second Mate's exams in the foc'stle or 'before the mast' which meant he had not served an apprenticeship. This is no criticism for the service was I suppose a meritocracy. Anyone with the correct amount of sea time could sit the exams and expect to make progress. Of course, shipping companies would tend to employ and favour their own men whom they knew to be reliable.

The Third Mate was not the usual young hopeful whom one might expect. He was probably getting on for sixty, rather short with grey curly hair and a magnificent grey walrus moustache. It was said that he had a 'Square Rigged Master's Ticket', that is he was an old sailing ship captain who no longer wanted responsibility and was content to 'see out his time'. He smoked hand rolled cigarettes made of Capstan Fine Cut flake tobacco, which were shaped rather like a megaphone. He was the type whom sailors referred to as 'an old shell back' but I came to call them the 'trilby hat brigade', for that was their favourite head gear. It was very practical too, since it kept the sun out of the eyes and the rain from going down the back of the neck.

I remember this Third Mate for three things. Although not on his watch I once had to answer his standby whistle and reported to him on the bridge. Not quite hearing what he said, I said "Pardon Sir?" With great indignation he drew himself up to his not very great height and in his rather cultured voice expostulated "You do not say pardon to me boy, just say Sir?" I never forgot. There was another occasion when we were at anchor off the Cape Verde Islands and we had a rope ladder over the side so that we could have a swim and splash around in the beautiful clear water. Suddenly it all went quiet. Everyone was looking up to the bridge where it could be seen that the old Third Mate, dressed in an ancient one piece swimming costume, was climbing through a bridge window on to the starboard light screen. He paused there for a while with arms raised to the front and then did a beautiful dive into the sea from about thirty or even forty feet I suppose. He then swam back to the ladder, climbed aboard and said not a word. The third event was during the war but I'll mention that later.

On these voyages from Europe to South America ships would usually call in either at the Canary Islands or the Cape Verde Islands on the way out and again when homeward bound. On the outward leg we would reach the Canaries in about ten days, the Cape Verdes being about two days further on. There we would top up with fuel oil, water, a few fresh vegetables and if we had money we would buy fruit from the 'bumboat' men. Just occasionally we might call in at Madeira or the Azores—what determined where we stopped I don't know except that at a certain time of the year we might load a deck cargo of tomatoes to bring home from Las Palmas in the Canaries.

One morning on the 'four to eight', as dawn was breaking but the sun was still below the horizon, we sailed past the high peak of Tenerife blazing in the sunlight without apparent means of support, for the lower flanks were still in darkness, a beautiful sight. This time we called in at St. Vincent in the Cape Verdes which was an old coaling station and which from the distant anchorage seemed quite barren. Small Negro children came out in rowing boats asking for pennies to be thrown into the sea so that they could dive and recover them.

Then came the long uninterrupted crossing of the South Atlantic, a run of between two and three weeks depending upon our destination. Good fine warm weather could be expected during this passage, promoting such comments as "People pay money to do this you know." Awnings would be put up on the forecastle head to keep down the temperature in the accommodation below. The Old Man would be seen sitting in a deck chair on the boat deck outside his cabin doing his paper work.

The Atlantic swells would get us rolling along and we new boys learned the skill of walking in a straight line on a moving deck. Very rarely there might be a line squall to disturb our serenity—a short sharp deep depression accompanied by a fierce wind and very heavy rain—the local name for them being 'Pampero' and then there was a mad dash to get the awnings in before they were carried away.

Time was occupied on this part of the voyage with inspecting and overhauling the cargo handling gear and of course any other maintenance. On this voyage we had an 'old' AB, probably in his fifties, who was another member of the trilby hat brigade. He was Irish, surnamed Murphy, but of course his real name was Paddy. Built like the proverbial barn door Paddy was ruggedly round faced, roughly shaven, and chewed tobacco—he always had a 'quid' and perhaps a little brown saliva escaping from the corner of his mouth.

Owing to his depth of experience Paddy was a 'day man'. In spite of his rough appearance he was as gentle as a lamb and had a beautiful character. He had been given the job of making a new towing spring or tow rope which was made of two parts, one of coir rope and the other of steel rope or hawser. The coir part was about four inches in diameter and had to have an eye spliced in to the towing end for the tug and a galvanised eye spliced in the other. Into the latter was spliced the steel hawser which was made fast on our 'bits' when on tow.

On my field day I was put to help Paddy, as it was a job that required more than one pair of hands. It took some time before I could understand him, his Irish brogue was so thick—there was not a 'th' in his vocabulary. After every exertion there would be an expectoration of brown liquid and "Der my boy, dats good." He was obviously very proud to be teaching the young apprentice how it should be done, and it was going to be done properly. All the equipment was laid out and all details planned and measured. Paddy was one of those men who look slow and ponderous but try and keep up with them and you find that because of their skill and economy of effort its difficult to do so. I learned a lot—we made a good job of it.

I had time during this passage to consider my position, both present and future—there is plenty of time for thought during two hours of lookout on the foc'stle head. The present was fine: I was well treated, well fed, I enjoyed the work, it was a man's world but the great thing was I was responsible for myself. I was beginning to see the shape of things and how the future might lie.

There was an organisation called The Merchant Navy Officers' Training Board and under its auspices a four-year syllabus had been drawn up indicating what an apprentice or cadet should study and revise during each year of service. In theory, if this study was followed the candidate would then be ready at the end of his time to sit the Board of Trade examination for Second Mate. Examinations were set annually by the Board. The B & S Line co-operated to the extent that we had to sit the examinations, although as far as I know no instructions were given to the officers to teach us or even to see that we did our studies—that was up to us. I was lucky in that later on Captain Owens did take an active interest in the progress of his apprentices.

I had discovered that there were also other ways into 'the profession'. The one I had taken was pretty well straight in at the deep end, but entrance was also possible via a training ship, of which I remember two. The Worcester I only remember by name but before I went to sea I remember the Conway being moored in the Mersey somewhere off Birkenhead and later during the war she would be moved to the Menai Straits. She was the 'hulk' of an old sailing ship, maybe one of the old 'wooden walls', a kind of residential nautical public school which was fee paying although there might have been scholarships. There was a strong RN influence and their cadets went either into the RN or the 'quality class' of merchant shipping company. Their cadets received a one-year reduction in the qualifying period of sea time if they did the two-year course.

I discovered too that on the completion of our apprenticeship it was the usual thing to attend a Nautical College or the Nautical Department of a Technical College for a period of a few weeks before taking the exams. The courses were of a twelve week repeating sequence and one had to be self financed to pay for course fees, exam fees, accommodation, the lot! This was a bit of a shock—where was the money to come from? There was not going to be much left from my apprenticeship wages of sixty pounds for the four years.

I learned that those who had no financial resources and did not want to get into debt often did a trip or two 'in the foc'stle' and saved up their wages. I resolved that I had better get down to serious studies so that I was well prepared when the time came. As it happened all was changed by the war and I encountered no problem but I was not to know that at the time. Finally, having acquired a Second Mate's 'Ticket' one then had to complete eighteen months (or was it two years?) of watch keeping sea time to sit for a First Mate's 'Ticket' and a further two years after that (or was it eighteen months?) to sit for 'Master'. That was often the end of the road, although for the ambitious or studious types there was also 'Extra Master's', a goal that seemed impossibly distant!

It was usual on this class of cargo ship for the officers to hold a Certificate of Competency one step above their rank ie. the third mate would hold a second mate's 'ticket', the second mate a first mate's and the first mate a master's ticket. One became a master through ability, reputation, seniority, maybe influence at the shipping company's office and perhaps by gaining extra master's.

Part of my equipment included three textbooks. One was Nicholl's Seamanship which in one edition covered almost everything except navigation—seamanship of course, engineering knowledge, ship construction, rule of the road, buoyage, signalling, cargo work, etc. etc. The second, Nicholl's Concise Guide Volume 1 was concerned with navigation (terrestrial and celestial), the trigonometric principles behind it and I think tidal calculations. The third volume was a book of tables—six figure logarithms, trig. ratios, traverse tables and many others. Although I had left school at the earliest opportunity I had had a good grounding at school in maths, logarithms, plane trigonometry and algebraic principles and since I found this fascinating it was for me a pleasure to learn. At the front of the text books was a suggested syllabus and pattern of work to follow. I wish I had the books now, they would be a fascinating bit of nostalgia. What happened to them I don't know, I probably dumped them when I left the sea because of their weight. (Since writing this I have indeed obtained copies of these books).

The weather got hotter and nothing is more pleasant than the South Atlantic when it's in a benign mood. 'The Line' was crossed with hardly a raised eyebrow, since to most people on board it was just routine. It became quite common to see shoals of flying fish skimming across the water and usually in the morning there would be a few dead ones lying around which had landed on deck during the darkness.

Just occasionally a land bird would alight on board and stay a day or two, whether they had been blown out to sea or merely resting on passage I never knew. Sea birds were common of course. In the Northern Hemisphere we would be accompanied by kittiwakes, petrels, terns or shearwaters skimming just over the wave tops and now and then flying through the spray off the crest of a wave. In the south the albatross would find us and stay for days while dolphins would swim and plunge off the bows. Occasionally whales could be seen 'spouting' in the distance.

There was the great black dome of starry sky, which slowly changed night after night. The well known stars and constellations of the northern sky disappeared and new ones appeared with intriguing names not heard of before or since—Capricorn, Sagittarius, Scorpio, Canopus and of course the Southern Cross.

The washtub came out and everyone got their laundry up to date. We youngsters who did not have a lot of gear had to do it rather more often than the older hands.

On one occasion when we were off but out of sight of the Brazilian coast we were enveloped in a vast cloud of large moths which clung everywhere. They had brown furry bodies about twenty-five mm. long and ten mm. diameter, a wingspan of perhaps fifty mm. I suppose they had been blown out to sea, They just wouldn't shift and in the end the Bosun had to get out the hoses and wash them away.

It was usually at about this time, ten days or so out from the Islands, that a change of diet occurred. With no refrigerator the fresh food gave out and we became dependant upon dried vegetables (peas and beans) and dried fruit (tinned fruit was very rare)—nice but never enough of it. Tinned and salted meat and salt fish appeared and rice replaced potatoes. In those days few people at home had refrigerators and so such food was not unknown to us, except for the salt meat and fish.

Some of the salt beef was quite nice although this really depended upon the skill and enterprise of the cook. I could never pretend to like the salt fish, which was one of the things the old shell backs would eat with gusto, but did they really like it? At the time of this change in diet the Chief Steward would, just before noon, put on number three hatch in front of the galley a white enamelled pail of diluted Rose's lime juice with a mug, from which all hands could help themselves. The Officers would also be supplied with a carafe on their dining table. The crew's rations were covered by BoT regulations and this was an anti scurvy one (shades of Captain Cook) and one of the reasons why British seamen all over the world were known as 'Limeys'.

Ships' cooks on vessels of our size were usually signed on as 'Cook and Baker' and a cook was very much judged by the quality of his bread—if that was good he could be forgiven other things. On one of the later voyages when we did have both a good cook and a good steward, something happened to the yeast and for a couple of days we had no bread and had to manage with ships biscuit to murmurs of appreciation from the old shell backs. Our resourceful steward was able to ferment some potato peelings in a large shallow bowl. I remember the white froth appearing on the top which the cook was able to use when baking and we had bread once again. It was rather grey in colour but better than the biscuit.

Friday was traditionally 'fish day'; Thursdays and Sundays were 'duff days'. That on Thursday would be white, such as a treacle pudding or spotted dick while on Sunday it would be plum duff, brown with dried fruit (but not a lot). Both were served with custard, rather lacking in cream but good filling stuff! I had already decided by this time that I preferred to drink my tea without milk rather than have it diluted with the tinned variety. Cold milkless sweet tea is good and thirst quenching in the tropics.

One unfortunate thing about the St. Merriel, and she was not alone in this, was that she was infested with brown and shiny cockroaches. There was really very little to be done about it except get used to it. Now and then, every twelve months or so, the crew would be sent to shore accommodation for a day and the ship was fumigated. It was effective for a while and when we returned on board there did not appear to be a living thing, but then I suppose the eggs hidden in cracks in the wood panelling would hatch out and after a while the insects would reappear, but only in darkness.

Some people tried ineffective means to control the pests. Remember that in those days there was no such thing as DDT, the only remedy we had was a spray called Flit. They would leave their cabin in darkness for a while and borrow the Flit spraygun. After a time the cabin door would be flung open, the light switched on and much vigorous pumping of the gun took place. There was some satisfaction in venting one's anger and frustration into the Flit gun but that was about all that was achieved. Some people had a more satisfying technique which was to keep an empty half pound tobacco tin and put a thin smear of butter around the inside just down from the rim. Foraging cockroaches would climb in but be unable to get out again because of the grease. They could be thrown overboard when there was a good harvest but a more sadistic and satisfying solution was to wait till the cook had left his galley and then tip them out on to the hot stovetop.

The galley was an important part of the ship for most crewmembers and not only because the food was prepared there. It ran across the fore part of our accommodation in front of the stokehold access and just behind number three hatch. A long rectangular room, it had steel barn type doors at both ends, beautifully made to smash or break any fingers that were in the way when the wind or roll of the ship swung them to—one became aware of these things. Running across its full width was a scrubbed beech worktop with cupboards and drawers beneath and two zinc lined sinks at one end, utensils hanging above.

Two cooking ranges ran along the opposite bulkhead. On one end stood a rectangular galvanised water tank, about three feet from front to back, two feet across and one and a half feet deep with a draw off tap at the end. This was the hot water supply for the whole ship, except for the engine room staff who had their own supply 'down below'. The cold water supply, again for the whole ship, was a hand operated lift pump (exactly the same as the one in the kitchen at Wyson) on the outside on the forrard galley bulkhead.

It was the firemen's responsibility to keep the galley bunker topped up with coal. When the galley boy was not on duty it was the watch keeping stand-by man who had to keep the hot water container topped up on the stove, the stoves fed with coal, and a large cast iron cooking pot had to be kept always 'on the simmer' for instant brews. On the rear galley bulkhead hung the iron fiddles, a collection of grid like fittings which could be put on the stove tops so that the saucepans, pans etc. would not slide about or even off if the ship was having a good roll. The cooking facilities were very basic by today's standards. At night-time the galley was a favourite refuge of the stand-by man since it was dry, warm and within hearing of the bridge whistle

All the lower deck crew had to visit the galley at some time or other every day, either for food or water or both, so it was quite a social meeting place. Much information, true and false, was exchanged there, to be disseminated on the 'Galley Wireless'. This became even more popular during the war when there was little in the way of real news and people would go up to the galley door and say "Watcha Cookie" or "Hello Doc, what d'you know?" Was he called Doc because he doctored the food?

If the cook was of a genial disposition there was usually quite a bit of banter going back and forth as the various messes queued up to collect their meals. Much of it was of a repetitive kind such as "Who called the cook a bastard?" to which someone would reply "Who called the bastard a cook?" Then, "He knows what he's about does our cook." and someone would reply "Oh yes, when it's brown it's cooked" and someone else would add the punch line "When it's black it's fucked!"

I recall that we did have a 'medicine chest' on board, which was a cupboard like a small pantry. Remedies for ailments were given out by the Chief Steward or sometimes the Second Mate—'black jack' or 'jollop' to help bowel movements, aspirin for most other things. We didn't suffer much from colds and sneezes, the fresh air saw to that. Any dentistry problems had to wait until we were in port and then it was 'out with the tooth'.

When the order came to get up the mooring ropes, cargo gear and rig the derricks we knew that land was not far away. Chippy broke out the anchor cable and as we got into sheltered waters the derricks were hoisted and the best quality hatch tarpaulins were made up and sent below. The aim was to have everything ready to start work as soon as we were alongside.

As hinted earlier, our peacetime commercial voyages, and indeed our early wartime ones followed the general pattern of discharging our cargo as we made our way down the coast of Brazil and then loading for home in Argentina. The Brazilian ports called at were known to us as Pernambuco (now marked on atlases as Recife), Maceio, Baia (Salvador), Rio de Janeiro the capital, Santos, Rio Grande du Sol, Porto Allegre and then perhaps Monte Video in Uruguay, in that order but not all of them on one voyage.

Some of the ports in those days were quite small—Maceio had no deep-water quays and we anchored off and discharged into lighters. Our first call on this voyage was Pernambuco and our stay was very short. We were only one night alongside and as one of the apprentices had to be on board I told Paul I was willing to stay and he could go ashore. As it happened a 'fiesta' was taking place and I remember him coming back aboard in the early hours of the morning almost incoherent with the excitement of having been dancing in the streets with the senoritas.

From there it was south to Rio and I was on stand by on the foc'stle head as we entered the harbour. No one who has sailed into that harbour for the first time can forget the experience. It was so dramatic passing through the narrow entrance into the huge bay surrounded by hills, beaches, and its modern city (this was sixty years ago). Prominent were its two special peaks, the Sugar Loaf and the Cocovada, a cable car running up to the former and a rack railway up to the latter with its summit crucifix floodlit at night.

Paul had somehow persuaded the Boatswain to show us the sights on our first night ashore, and we were to be ready for eight o'clock. At the appointed hour two taxis arrived—we were a party of seven or eight—and I remember that coming from the car radio in our taxi was the overture from the Rossini opera 'The Barber of

Seville', which seemed so appropriate for the dark starry night on this warm evening in a Latin American country.

I had no idea what was in store but I'm sure Paul did, that was the reason we were there, and eventually somewhere out in the suburbs we left the taxis and entered a large, spacious and tastefully furnished bungalow where we were welcomed by the Madame. It was a brothel! Beer was ordered—I had never tasted beer before—we sat on the various chairs and settees and in trouped a band of young, nicely turned out senoritas. If one's idea of such a place is somewhere dark, dowdy and furtive, then this was not it. It had class.

Up until then I had rather put the opposite sex on a pedestal, which I suppose reflected the way I had been brought up. I liked girls; I liked their company and had enjoyed mild flirtations with girls who, as far as I knew, were 'chaste'. To have a beautifully if flimsily clad young female sit on my knee, put her hand on my vital parts and whisper in my ear "Fucky fuck Johnny?" was shattering.

I was not prepared for such an experience, remember I was still only sixteen and sex was not brazened about in those days as it is today. If someone had taught her to say "Hello sailor, would you like to come to bed with me?" it would have been a bit more seductive. I recovered, but not sufficiently to accept the offer, and in any case I had no money. When it was obvious that that was so, like a true professional she lost interest. During the course of the night other venues were visited but I remember only that one in any detail.

Therein lay the plight of cadets and apprentices; we were poor, very poor if relying simply on our earnings as most of us were. We were probably about five weeks into the voyage so by then, at rather less than four shillings weekly, I had about one pound on the books. One could not afford the life of a libertine. On a later trip, when I was older and did have spare cash, I would visit the Copacabana beaches and take the train to the top of the Cocovada but I never liked Rio—it was a big city!

Our next stop was a small riverside port called Santos where we arrived in the late afternoon. There wasn't a berth available. South American ports were busy in those days with shipping visiting from all over the world, from the USA to Japan but with much of it

British, and we anchored off in the river using two anchors.

The Mate, the Old Man, or I suppose both must have decided that I was reliable enough to carry some responsibility. Sea watches had ended and I was to go on night anchor watch—all night—and I had already been up since four in the morning! The Mate took me up on to the foc'stle head, explained that this was a tidal river and that it would change from flow to ebb at about two thirty in the morning. The ship was being held on the port anchor but as the tide turned she would swing and the weight would be taken up on the starboard cable. The reason for the two anchors was to limit the area of swing so as not to foul other ships anchored nearby. We should all swing the same way at the same time. He explained how by putting one's hand on the cable one could feel the vibrations of a dragging anchor and then he took me up on to the bridge to show how to take a bearing on a shore mark which should remain constant. If it did not and if I was at all worried I was to call him immediately.

I was to switch on the anchor light at dusk, clip it on the halyard and hoist it up the forestay. At dawn I was to lower it down and replace it with the 'black ball' (the regulation daylight signal for a ship at anchor, it was not really a ball but two circular discs at right angles to each other, hoisted on the fore part of the vessel). I should call Paul to relieve me at six in the morning and I would then be free till six in the evening when I would continue as night watchman. The steward had instructions to leave me a plate of sandwiches and brews of tea.

It was not the only night I spent on anchor watch at Santos but it was certainly the most anxious one, if only because it was the first and worried me greatly. I was constantly taking bearings and examining the cables but of course there was little enough to worry about really—if there had been I wouldn't have been given the job.

Situated just south of the Tropic of Capricorn, Santos as I remember it was on the south side of a river that was quite wide at that point, the river entrance being much narrower and on one steep hillside was an enormous CINZANO sign. As dawn broke the river would always be covered in mist. It was quite a long lasting dawn for the sun had to climb above the surrounding hills, but eventually it would break clear and the mist would be dispelled. On the northern side all appeared to be forested. The water was often like glass but it could be swift flowing at full ebb. As it became light the birds we knew as 'Bromliekites' (which may have been an invention, as was 'Shitehawks', the other name by which we knew them) would appear, diving down and skimming along the water, to catch with their feet anything which they thought edible, in the same manner as the sea eagle. Occasionally, a group of them would dive in line ahead as the Stuka dive bombers were to do later on. Sailors carrying food from the galley to their mess always covered the mess tins with a cloth. The Shitehawks had the reputation for carrying off more than one sailor's dinner.

I quite liked Santos, which though busy was quite small. A tram service ran alongside the docks so that it was easy to get to town, or it was not too far to walk if one was so inclined. It was at that time the largest exporter of coffee in the world and the smell from the quayside coffee warehouses was marvellous. There was a quite nice Flying Angel Seamen's Mission in town where one could sit, relax and read an old newspaper or magazine. It had a piano and our cabin boy, a first tripper like me, was one of those gifted people who could play anything by ear. He was in love with Dianna Durbin and had seen the film 'One Hundred Men and a Girl' so many times that he knew Liszt's Hungarian Rhapsody off by heart and he would rattle it off as soon as we got there. The Mission had another great advantage—it was free. I was amazed to see recently on the internet pictures showing how Santos has changed into a modern city, complete with acres of 'skyscrapers'.

One drawback of the Brazilian coastal ports was the mosquito population. It was too hot to sleep covered by bedclothes and too hot to keep the portholes closed. Being fair skinned I seemed to gather more than my fair share of irritant bites around the ankles, neck, wrists and forearms. I suppose a mosquito net would have been the answer but we didn't have such luxuries.

From there it was on down to the River Plate and Buenos Aires. Approaching the estuary one became aware first of the change in the water colour as the blue of the ocean turned to the light brown of the outflowing fresh water. If one was approaching in the morning at the time of a strong ebb, the second thing noticeable was all the refuse from upriver on its way out to sea, including thousands of 'French letters' as they were then called—condoms today—and this was a Roman Catholic country! I believe all large estuaries have the same characteristic. It was quite a long haul up river from picking up the pilot and as beginners Paul and I were not allowed to steer but our time would come later.

At 'BA' we completed discharging which included those long steel rails that had been lying in the after holds since Antwerp. As the holds were emptied so they were swept out and cleaned up, much of this being done during our passages from port to port. The worst part of this was getting rid of the waste cement from torn and broken bags. For obvious reasons we couldn't wash it away or even damp it down and the floating dust in the holds was appalling.

Buenos Aires, like Rio, was a capital city with all its size, bustle and vices. Stretching away from the docks towards the city was a long line of bars, brothels disguised as dance halls, sex shows etc. designed to please the visiting sailors and anyone else for that matter, and relieve them of their money as quickly as possible. From what I remember they seemed to be installed under an overhanging roadway and were infamously known as 'The Arches', as indeed they were. The most notable building in town at that time was the Casa Rosa, the pink stoned presidential palace, from which Eva Peron would eventually harangue the mob. I didn't like BA. I didn't like the police—they did not look customer friendly.

We were by this time 'light ship' with much of the hull out of the water. As many seamen as could be spared were sent overside on 'stages' to chip and scrape away rust and barnacles and to paint with red lead and red boot-topping the plates that were normally under water. I must mention here that the Bosun mixed our own red lead, white lead and white zinc paints from the basic ingredients and by tradition he always peed in the red lead—it was supposed to improve its durability, but that probably depended on the state of the Bosun.

We apprentices did not take part in the activity of painting the hull, the Mate was much concerned in getting the holds ready for the next cargo and we were his right hand men. Limber boards that covered the bilges had to be lifted and the bilges cleaned out if necessary. This could be a filthy stinking job as the refuse and detritus from previous cargoes gathered there and condensation would trickle down into them from the hull plates and rot it. This was traditionally an apprentice's job. It was, however, never too bad on the St. Merriel, probably because the Mate insisted the bilges were cleaned out every time we could gain access. Also he was most insistent that the limber boards were put back as they should be, and that if we were to carry grain these boards were properly covered with hessian.

From BA we went up river to Rosario in Argentina, about a days steaming, to load the bulk grain part of our homeward cargo. There seemed to be little there to get enthusiastic about. The grain was tipped into the holds down shutes from railway wagons. Frequently the ship had to be shifted along by hauling on the mooring ropes so that the shutes could get access to another hold. Frequently (so it seemed) this happened at unfriendly hours like six o'clock in the morning or seven at night, and it was all so dusty.

Grain can be a dangerous cargo if not loaded properly, it tends to settle leaving a gap at the top of the hold and if the ship then rolls past the 'angle of repose' the whole lot can run sideways causing a shift in the centre of gravity. Ships have capsized in such cases. There were BoT regulations that had to be observed, with some ships erecting shifting boards and feeders. The technique practised on the St. Merriel was to load three quarters of the grain in bulk and then when back in BA to top this up with grain in sacks. At this time the Mate would be seen in his white boiler suit lying on his side with a long handled wooden rake making sure that the grain was well trimmed out to the sides with no voids. It was a job he always did himself.

Whilst that went on the stages went over the side again and the black topsides of the hull were painted. The ship's name and port of registry were renewed in white. The seamen would have a last fling ashore to get rid of their remaining pesos and then we were away with about four weeks of sailing in front of us. It was stow away, wash down, and paint, paint, paint all the way home from the top of the masts to the black steel deck and everything in between.

The fair South Atlantic weather enabled us to do a good job in comfort. The Saint Line colour scheme was 'mast colour' for the masts, samson posts, derricks and ventilators, which was a kind of dark 'Stork Margarine' colour, with white for the deck houses, accommodation blocks and bridge with black detailing. The red funnel had a black top, below which on either side was the company house flag, at that time a white background with a red diagonal cross. This is the flag of St. Patrick I think but what he had to do with a Welsh shipping company I don't know. (I think maybe he lived in Wales before going to 'save' the Irish or was it the other way round?)

A couple of trips later I returned from leave to see these metal 'flags' had been taken down to have a shield installed in the centre. I learned that this was the coat of arms of Lord Howard de Walden, reputedly the largest landowner in the country, who had bought his way into the company. They looked quite posh and the company officially now became The South American Saint Line by which it was already known colloquially.

On the way to the UK we called in at the Canaries and then it was across the Bay, up the Channel and the East Coast to the Humber and the port of Kingston upon Hull to discharge.

During the four and a half months since joining the ship I had earned about three pounds ten shillings and maybe I had spent a half of this, which did not leave enough for a rail ticket home. As it happened only one of the apprentices could go on leave: Paul wanted to see his girl friend so I said I would stay. Mother and Dad decided they would come up to Hull for a few days to see me.

So ended the first voyage. I suppose I have remembered so much of it because everything that happened was the first experience. If the details have gone on too long in some places I'm sorry but my intention is to write a true record rather than a dramatised or exaggerated account.

5

OUTBREAK OF WAR

The Convoy System

Leaving Hull in May 1939, it was over to Antwerp again. This cycle of voyages of three to four months duration to known destinations, with predicted times of arrival and departure, was what made employment with companies like the Saint Line attractive to married men. They were able to keep up a regular written correspondence with their wives and take leave at regular intervals. I enjoyed these voyages too but there were times when I would have preferred to be on a tramp going anyplace, anywhere, since I was still unattached.

Whilst the first voyage remains clear to me and I was to make six more on the St. Merriel, those that followed tend to blur together so that what follows are incidents from those voyages which are only more or less in chronological order. The dates of these voyages are written on the back of my Indentures, which I think would have been done by someone in the Company office where the Indentures were held.

The second voyage differed from the first in two respects. When we got to Antwerp the crew, excepting officers, engineers, sparks, the Chief Steward and the Boatswain, paid off and returned to the UK. In their places we signed on a crew from the Antwerp shipping office, many of them being what we now call Eastern Europeans. They were mostly Hungarians, Bulgarians, and Rumanians. Chippy was Norwegian. Strangest of all the Galley Boy was a bald headed Armenian who must have been in his late thirties. Knowing no better, I suppose, I just accepted this and took it as normal but I have often wondered since what it was that brought these disparate people to Belgium to sign on a British ship. Was it simply that they needed employment or was it the result of politics? Whatever it was they were good seamen and good workers, all speaking English to some extent with some having a number of languages, and they were never any cause of trouble or indiscipline.

The other incident of note occurred when we were almost ready to leave Buenos Aires on the return part of my second voyage whereupon the Galley Wireless reported that we were to take passengers! Unlike some of the newer ships in the Company we did not have passenger accommodation so how could this be so? Later bulletins said that the two spare cabins in the officers' accommodation were to be used, one of which was labelled 'Hospital' and that it was a missionary family going to the UK on furlough.

So it was they came on board the day before we left with a whole host of people to see them off. It was soon established that there was mum, dad, a daughter of about sixteen and two boys of about seven, although we were really too busy to take much notice. After sailing they disappeared for a few days, probably getting their sea legs and then they began to appear, relaxing on the Old Man's boat deck. There were two ways up to the bridge, port side and starboard, that on the starboard side going past the Old Man's accommodation and no one went that way, except by invitation to see the Old Man, or if the weather was so atrocious that the port side was impassable with safety. He had obviously thought it was his duty to offer them the use of his private domain.

By this time I had become quite handy with a paintbrush and was often given jobs that required a bit of care. One morning when I reported to the Bosun for my field day he gave me a pot of black paint and what we called a cutting in brush, small and flat, and sent me to paint the grab rail and fittings on the foreside of the bridge accommodation block. I had almost completed the task when a round faced female blonde head popped out of the porthole above and said, "Hello, what are you doing?" although of course that was pretty obvious.

It transpired that her name was Muriel and whilst the family was in the UK she was to go to Malvern Girls' School for twelve months or so. She was a pleasant extrovert sort of girl getting bored with inactivity and an all adult society, and I suspect that Captain Owens, who had an artful side to his character, had suggested that he had a couple of apprentice officers who would be pleased to entertain her and pointed us out to her. I suggested to her that I could make up some rope quoits and after the midday meal, when some of our younger members were off watch or off duty, we could make up a game of deck quoits or deck tennis. Later that is what we did and it became hilarious at times when the ship had a good roll on and many quoits went over the side.

At eleven o'clock when I went aft to turn in my pot of paint and clean the brush—and to scrounge some rope off the Bosun—I found him with a can of turps substitute and quantities of cotton waste trying to clean up her younger brothers. They had asked him for a job. Fastened to the after deck was the 'kedge', a large old-fashioned Admiralty type anchor. He had given them a can of black paint and a small brush each and suggested they paint it. They had, very enthusiastically. As they had crawled around under and over to get at all the nooks and crannies they had got black paint all over themselves and their overalls. Although they had enjoyed themselves tremendously, the Bosun appeared to be a bit worried.

Eventually the weather turned against us and put an end to our deck games. Approaching the Channel we ran into thick fog. This was before the days of radar and satellite navigation and our only way of getting a good fix was by celestial navigation or a sight of landmarks, so no sun, moon, stars, or horizon meant no fix! On 'Monkey Island', a small structure above the bridge, was a direction finding aerial from which it should have been possible to obtain bearings of certain radio stations, but it was treated with derision by the Old Man and the officers. Later on when I was older and 'practising' navigation the Third Mate and I once tried to use it but got no results at all.

The International Rules for the Prevention of Collisions at Sea said that in fog and bad visibility ships should go at a moderate speed, giving a prolonged blast on the steam whistle or siren every two minutes. This we did and Captain Owen's interpretation of a moderate speed was to go at half speed with the engine room telegraph on 'Standby'. It is a great strain peering into impenetrable fog and listening for the hoot of another ship, one could never be certain from what direction the sound came, all one could do then was to reduce speed to dead slow and 'feel' one's way past.

After about three days of this had passed there was another worry as the officers were not sure of our position anymore. For the first and only occasion during my time on the St. Merriel we rigged and used the 'deep sea lead,' a large leaden weight on the end of a steel wire, which was lowered from the end of a swung out boom with a hand winch whilst the ship was stationary (we did not have then what later became commonplace technology, an 'echometer' or 'fathometer' that told the depth of water under the keel). The purpose, I was told, was to see if we had yet reached the Continental Shelf that sweeps out from the northern end of the Bay of Biscay and up the West Coast of Ireland like a platform, on which stands the British Isles. What the result of all this effort was I don't remember, only the event.

Slowly the fog lifted and I remember one of the Rumanian seamen pointing out to me a couple of French and British destroyers at exercise out in the mist but I failed at the time to see the significance of this.

This weather was not untypical. After some time away we would be looking forward to seeing England's green and pleasant land again, only to be greeted with a world of greyness. Any excitement generated at this time, through being near to the UK at the end of the voyage, was known as 'Channel Fever'. Less politely, it was also referred to as 'the kiss my arse latitudes', the suggestion there being that those who had decided to pay off at the end of the voyage and were not worried about being asked to make another trip were likely to be a little 'sans souci' in the way they performed their duties. During the voyage on the first of June 1939 I passed my seventeenth birthday but the event would have gone by unnoticed. We continued up Channel to Hull.

I went home for a few days leave. It was strange. I remember, and it was always to be so, how I then felt very different from the few friends I had left behind and I felt conscious that people I knew were observing me closely to see in what way I had changed. I have to say that at times I thought, 'If only they knew'.

My third voyage began in mid August 1939 when there was talk of war and preparations for war. I can't remember us 'young ones' taking this very seriously as we didn't get a lot of 'news' when at sea, but our minds were concentrated a bit when we got to Antwerp. Paul went ashore on the Saturday evening to a dance at the Seamen's Mission. There he met two girls—'nice' girls—one of whom he fancied and asked to see the next afternoon, Sunday, but she would only agree if her friend was included. Would I go? Well of course I would and we got the Mate's permission for us both to be off the ship.

I remember two things very clearly. We went for afternoon tea in what I thought was a very nice large circular restaurant. After a while I looked around and was surprised to see myself sitting on the other side of the room. The room was semicircular and the straight diameter was a mirror wall! Secondly what started as a bright, animated and somewhat flirtatious occasion—they spoke a little more English than we did French—slowly turned to melancholy. They were far more conversant with European affairs than we were, and although hoping fervently that there would not be a war, they were convinced that Hitler's Germany was predatory. They thought that war was almost inevitable, with dire consequences for Belgium. They were right of course. We took them to their tram stop promising to see them again next time. There was to be no next time and I've often wondered what happened to them.

Our Stornaway Bosun had left us and in his place came an Estonian, a smallish man with a rather military bearing who spoke very good English and was quite efficient. There were other minor changes. The Hebrideans had gone but the main body of seamen stayed with us, which was a good sign.

There were no more opportunities to go ashore and we sailed on the last day of August. The Old Man must have been given his instructions, for on the way down the Scheldt the Bosun mixed some extra thick black paint with which we painted over all the portholes, glass and brassware. Electric light bulbs were taken out of all rooms and alleyways that opened to the outside and canvas screens were made up and fixed across alleyway entrances so that the doors inside could be opened without any light showing. We had 'blacked out'—things looked ominous!

War was declared on Sunday the third of September 1939 as we broke out of the Channel. What we didn't know was that submarines and commerce raiders were already out there waiting. What the Old Man knew was his secret. He must have been briefed but his information was not passed down to underlings. We became aware of what war really meant on Monday when we heard that the Athenia had been torpedoed to the north of us, but I can't remember whether Sparks had heard their S O S or whether we heard about it from a news bulletin.

I should explain about the 'Sparkies'. Although they signed on the Ship's Articles and were subject to the Master's discipline, they were actually employees of a wireless company, which was usually Marconi but could have also been EMI. The equipment and operators (by courtesy Radio Officers) were supplied by the radio company under contract to the shipping company and on ships like ours there was just one of them. They kept a watch schedule according to International Regulations.

By general request, when the war started Sparks listened to the BBC news and wrote out a short daily newssheet. Radio silence was now imposed except for emergencies, when a series of SSSs signalled a ship was under attack by submarine, a series of RRRs by a commerce raider and AAAs meant by aircraft. Later on we would have three operators on a ship keeping a continuous watch. We were not allowed to have or use portable radios for fear that they would give out emissions that could be picked up and located by the enemy. Bizarrely, there was even the same restriction on electric shavers!

Next day, Tuesday 5th September, was the third day of the war. Shortly after I took over first wheel on the four to eight p.m. watch the Old Man came up the bridge ladder with a piece of paper in his hand and went into the chart room. He emerged soon after to tell the Mate that Sparks had heard an S O S from the Royal Sceptre that had been attacked and sunk by a U-boat. Their position was twenty-three miles astern of us—we had passed through that position only two hours before!

Thinking about it now I am just amazed that this event made so little difference to us. Ship's routine carried on as though this was just a normal peacetime voyage. In peacetime the daylight watch had comprised two men on the bridge: the Officer of the Watch and the Helmsman. At night-time an additional seaman had acted as lookout. This lookout still came off duty when it became daylight leaving it all to do by the Officer of the watch, which was all right during peacetime but we really should have kept a seaman on too, preferably located as high up as possible. It's obvious that we had no idea of the threat that was out there. (I have since read that the Royal Sceptre was an armed merchant cruiser but that is an error—she was not. In any case she was the third ship to be sunk in the war).

Where we did differ from peacetime routine was that at night-time we now sailed without navigation lights, in fact in utter darkness with not even cigarettes allowed. In a reversal of normal procedure we were painting ship on the outward voyage. The Bosun had made his own version of 'battleship grey' by mixing the stock of white and black paint that we carried—although the shade turned out to be rather dark.

We realised how important this was later on when in the early convoys some neutral ships were included, still with their super-structures painted white. They stood out quite alarmingly on moon-lit nights but this was soon rectified—since they could only go by convoy they had to conform. At some time during the subsequent

South American voyages the decor changed and the upper works on most ships was painted all over mast colour (a margarine shade), but afterwards we reverted to grey again.

Nothing more untoward happened on the outward voyage. The South American discharging and loading proceeded as usual, but times of arrival and departure were kept secret—supposedly! Its likely that all dockland knew them better than we did.

On completion and ready to sail for home the Old Man received his instructions to proceed to Freetown on the West African coast of Sierra Leone. (This was to be our future assembly port for homeward convoys; no more did we use the Canaries. Two German tankers which were at Las Palmas at the outbreak of the war remained and secretly refuelled U-boats).

Calculating back from the time of our arrival in the UK, we must have left the River Plate in the first half of December 1939. It was on December 13th. that the British cruisers trapped the German pocket battleship Graf Spee off Rio and on the 17th. when she scuttled at Monte Video. We must have left by then. Since she had travelled from the waters off South Africa our paths must have crossed somewhere in the South Atlantic.

A number of the ships that the Spee had sunk were on the same trade as us and known to us, as were some of the crews who were put on the Altmark, one of her supply ships. They were eventually rescued by British matelots from the destroyer Cossack lead by Captain Vian who boarded the Altmark in Norwegian waters on her way to Germany. Later in the war when we had loaded for the Sicilian invasion, my ship was 'inspected' by Admiral Vian—I was thrilled. (Even later, on holiday in Norway, Edna and I made a sentimental journey to Jossing Fjord where the rescue took place and I took an evening photograph of the commemoration stone).

We arrived at Freetown where there gathered merchant ships from South America, Africa, and when the Mediterranean was closed to traffic from the East, New Zealand and Australia as well. Not an attractive place was Freetown.

I was still only a young apprentice and not privy to important decisions, but I know there was a lot of apprehension amongst the

officers and the Old Man at having to sail in convoy in close prox-
imity to other ships. The reaction of most Captains when they saw
another ship was to keep well out of the way.

We had little in the way of equipment, certainly no daylight signalling lamps. We could semaphore with flags of course. We had the
flags of the International Code of Signals, which would be used for
general signals and Chippy made up a flag locker, which he installed
on the bridge so that we had the flags stored in alphabetical order
and handy. I say 'we' because the apprentices were going to be relied on to do quite a bit of the signalling. Unlike the Royal Navy we
did not carry specialist signalmen. Flag halliards were rigged on the
foremast yardarms and passed to either side of the bridge.

The voice pipe from the bridge to the engine room was tested
to check that they could hear instructions regarding speed—they
could if they were shouted loud enough. Calculations were made
to estimate what engine revolutions coincided with what speed
through the water and that was about it as regards to preparations.

The Old Man and the Second Mate went ashore at the appointed time to the convoy conference but little of what took place
was passed down to us underlings. I don't think we had a proper
Convoy-Signalling Book at this time, just a few duplicated pages on
the chart room table. The authorities ashore drew up a plan of the
convoy.

Upon leaving Freetown, these convoys were usually from nine
to perhaps a dozen or more columns in width, four and occasionally five ships in a column. The stations were numbered from the
port (or left) front corner, the number of the column first so that
23 would be the third ship in the second column and 71 the leading ship of the seventh column. Leading the centre would be the
Commodore in one of the ships that carried passengers, say one of
Ellerman's or the United Africa Company's. He was usually a retired
senior naval officer who had a small staff with him including his RN
signallers.

Early convoys were a bit chaotic to start with—every one was
suspicious of everyone else's intentions and capabilities. On sailing day all ships would shorten cable so as to be able to get under

way quickly and at the appointed hour ships would fly their station number pennants and ensigns. The Commodore would steam slowly out of the anchorage, followed theoretically in the prescribed order by all others in two columns, those with a station nearest to him first. He would probably be flying the flags K5, which meant a convoy speed of five knots, and was meant to be slow enough to enable ships to catch up with him and take station. In the early days its likely that a few old ships would be near to bursting their boilers at eight knots so it would be hours before everyone was in place. Some of them probably never got there and had to chance it on their own. It was intended that there should be three cables or six hundred yards between columns and two cables between ships in line, so even if all kept tight station a convoy could be three or four miles across.

Outside the escort would be waiting. In this first instance it was one of the Union Castle liners fitted out as an AMC, that is to say she had been fitted with half a dozen WW1 six-inch guns and called an Armed Merchant Cruiser. She looked huge and had been painted in two shades that were more mauve than grey—not for them an Estonian Bosun's mix. Even this meagre escort was better than nothing since in that part of the world at the time we were more likely to be accosted by a commerce raider than by submarines, and a couple of the AMCs did truly heroic service.

Keeping station was at that time 'beyond the ken' of Merchant Service personnel. It was not too difficult 'across the width'. On the convoy plan with the name and position of every ship was the height of the top of its mainmast above the water line. It was quite easy to find from tables the angle at which to set a sextant to get the correct distance off, but one had to keep in line and if the leading ship steered an erratic course it was difficult.

It was errors in speed that caused most problems. A steady speed required a steady steam pressure from the boilers. In the oil burning St. Merriel that was not difficult, where with three burners to a boiler they could be turned off or flashed up quite readily although it took time to build up or let down pressure.

The real problem was with some of the old coal burners. To get a place in the convoy, maybe with a little pride at stake, some captains would give their ship's speed as say nine knots whereas it would be lucky to do eight with a clean bottom on good Welsh steaming coal. With doubtful coal and a weedy bottom they didn't stand a chance. At the end of a watch when traditionally fires were raked, cleaned and banked some of these ships seemed almost to come to a stop and rapidly fell astern. Some of them never caught up and some of them never lived to tell the tale.

Another engine room routine that had to be changed was 'blowing the tubes' of our boilers which sent clouds of black soot and smoke skywards from the funnel, an absolute give away to enemy lookouts. This now had to be done under cover of darkness. RN ships had water tube boilers that enabled steam pressure to be controlled much more rapidly, but unlike us they were not built for economical running.

Another hazard of the early days was caused by some of the diesel engined motor ships that had a critical speed at which the engine and everything else with it vibrated to an extent that it became dangerous. If this coincided with the convoy speed such ships would get permission from the Commodore to take a position between columns and then cruise up and down until the convoy speed changed.

Probably many masters had little sleep that first night but as dawn broke next day all was well and there was our escort zigzagging majestically back and forth ahead of the convoy. The station keeping got better with experience and within a few days the Commodore was exercising us at emergency turns where the whole convoy at a signal turned together perhaps forty five degrees to port or starboard and stayed so for an hour or more. It was always interesting to see who was where when we got back on the original course.

A more protracted manoeuvre was altering course in succession when the ships on the 'inside of the bend' had to slow down and those on the outside had to belt away as fast as they could to catch up on station. It used to take ages. Some captains were reluctant to leave the bridge in the charge of junior officers but they got used to it. Later on in the war, sometimes a complete convoy would zigzag in time together. Then one had to be on the alert in case some dozy helmsman went the wrong way!

It must have been soon after this that I was called to Captain Owens's cabin. He told me that he had our first year exam papers in his safe and that he had arranged with the Chief Steward that the saloon would be kept free for us during the afternoons of the following week, each exam to start at two o'clock—in our own time!

Our convoy 'proceeded without incident'. Somewhere out in the ocean but much nearer to home we met up with our close escort comprising a couple of destroyers and a few naval oddments. They had brought out a convoy that had dispersed on its way and were to take us back in. We eventually took a coastal convoy through the Channel and up to Hull.

It must have been December 1939 or January 1940. I went home on leave and so did Paul but I doubt if it was a very happy time for him. In one of the South American ports a senorita had bestowed upon him more favours than he would have wished and he had 'caught a dose' of gonorrhoea. This was before the days of penicillin or so called M&B tablets and the treatment on ship was by irrigation—I can't remember with what but it was certainly a long and fairly miserable process. He also had to have his own eating and washing utensils so in a way it was a bit like being ostracised. It affected his personality; he became withdrawn and didn't want to talk. When he got home he would have to see his doctor and maybe visit a VD Clinic. What happened to his relationship with his much talked of girl friend I don't know. I never saw or heard of him again. It was quite sad. No doubt he thought of me as being staid and serious, and I certainly thought of him as being immature and irresponsible, but we had got on well together.

My leave was different. On the evening of the second day I went to see my old friend Jack Plum and was greeted with the news that he had started 'courting' and was to meet his girl friend when she came out of the St. John's Ambulance class at nine o'clock. "Never mind" said Jack, "there will be other girls there".

We were outside the Town Hall waiting when the girls came out. Jack met up with Gladys, introduced me and with what turned out to be great prescience said, "Where's Edna? Go and fetch her!" which she did. Again I was introduced and soon there was a group of about six or seven of us standing chatting away. It was January, pitch dark of course, complete blackout, no lights, but I liked the little I could see and hear of Edna, so before anything further could happen I said "I'll take this young lady home!" She did not demur and she agreed to see me again the next day! I remember that Jack thought this significant because of the number she had refused. I found her to be even more attractive in the daylight!

We agreed to write to each other and so began five years of courtship by correspondence and not very regular correspondence at times. There would be periods when we could not send or receive letters for weeks, then perhaps four or five would arrive together. It was necessary to number them so that they could be read in the correct sequence and one could tell if any were missing. Although Edna and I were unknown to each other then, we were not total strangers in that we had both been to the same school but were not in the same class, she had been a year ahead of me but neither of us remembered the other.

6

MAN OVERBOARD!

But a hard landing

Leave did not last very long. Returning to the St. Merriel after being on board for a year was like going home, but what changes there were! The after steering house had been strengthened and on the top two guns were mounted, both First World War vintage of course. One we learned was a four inch semi-automatic for surface firing and the other a twelve-pounder artillery piece on a high angle mounting for anti aircraft use.

An electric bell system had been installed to communicate with the engine room—long rings to indicate an increase in engine speed, short ones a decrease—so that two long rings meant increase by two revolutions, four short ones decrease by four and so on.

Eventually there arrived Joe, the RN gunner, a chirpy Cockney who had done his thirteen years and been placed on the reserve. On mobilisation he had been recalled and had volunteered for DEMS service (Defensively Equipped Merchant Ships, mentioned later). He was in his thirties and on leaving the Navy had trained as a plumber. (He taught me how to 'wipe a joint', which came in useful many years later).

Since Paul hadn't returned there came a new apprentice.

Surnamed Rogers, he was never known as anything else, unless it was something abusive. Straight out of some minor public school, he turned out to be a bit of a twit, very keen but a bit stupid. Joe had to have somewhere to live so he was put into Paul's old cabin and Rogers had to move in with me. He was amenable and since we were on different watches we did not see a great deal of each other. He always did what I told him without demur but nobody had taught him the old maxim for a youngster of 'Hear all, see all and say nowt' and consequently he was always getting into hot water.

From then on the pattern of our trade slowly changed. There were for us no longer any trips to Antwerp. What the British did have to offer for export at that time was coal, so having discharged at Hull we were sent to one of the South Wales ports to load. Loading coal is a filthy task. Invariably one moors alongside tower like structures where railway wagons are hoisted, tipped, and forty tons of black coal and dust pours into the hold—but not all of the dust, a lot of it just wafts around and settles any and every where; doors may be shut and portholes screwed down but still it gets through.

It can be a dangerous cargo too. Ships have caught fire or even exploded through spontaneous combustion caused by the correct ventilation not being observed. It's not a very pleasant job cleaning out the holds afterwards—the dust rises in the air in clouds so that it's impossible to see more than a couple of yards. Eyes, nostrils and lips become encrusted with a black rim. On this occasion in January 1940 it must have been very cold and snowy for when we were later to discharge at Santos the stevedores were to complain bitterly—the small coal in the middle of number four hold was frozen together!

The convoy assembly port for the Bristol Channel was Milford Haven. From there we were to be escorted out into the Atlantic for a hundred miles or so beyond Ireland to longitude twelve and a half degrees west, whereupon the outward convoy would disperse and the escort would rendezvous with an inward bound convoy. Escorts were still a bit thin on the water in those days, perhaps one destroyer or maybe two, they were being held back for fear of invasion. It was at this time that we first heard, and saw depth charges being detonated. We were quite impressed and wished our escort every success.

As soon as we sailed it was made known that volunteers were needed for the four inch gun crew and Joe told me that the Mate had suggested that I should volunteer to be sight setter, which I was pleased to do. Joe was gunlayer and actually pressed the trigger, the chief steward was trainer who traversed the gun. I can't remember who was breach worker but the loader was appropriately the cook, name of Louis Gould.

I say appropriately because Louis was a good amateur boxer going back to schoolboy days, and with his flattened nose he looked like one. Louis looked to be quite a toughy but he was one of the gentlest of men. He had two pairs of sparring gloves with him and he used to give us instruction in the noble art—how to lead, jab, cross, parry, cover and so on. I did all right until hit on the nose and then my eyes watered so much that I couldn't see, it happened every time! I don't think there is anything more exhausting than boxing. There was a large Seamen's Mission in BA with a weekly boxing night and Louis would sometimes give an exhibition match with one of the locals.

Being an 'Old Stripey' (so named after the long service stripes worn on the sleeve, three for longest service), Joe trained us to do everything by the book. On the order "Load!" the supply party would dump a shell and cartridge case—dummies of course—on the loading tray and Louis would swing it up to the breach. Wearing a padded glove like a knuckle-duster he would ram them up the spout as though he was delivering a right to the solar plexus. My job as sight setter was to manipulate two graduated wheels that adjusted the sights for range and deflection as called out by the gunnery officer, in our case the Second Mate, who I suppose had taken a gunnery course. These were laid on at all major UK ports, attendance entirely voluntary. At first we practised every afternoon and soon got a good rhythm going; thereafter we practised twice a week.

One evening at dusk the Commodore hoisted the signal to disperse at a given time and as dawn broke the next morning we were alone. The Old Man opened his sealed instructions giving the route we were to take, this being in the form of latitude and longitude positions through which we had to pass. I suppose this was so that the Admiralty knew more or less where we were, to keep our shipping dispersed and if they had the intelligence information, to keep us away from known surface raiders. This meant that we sometimes traversed areas well away from the normal shipping lanes.

Sometimes far to the west edging the Sargasso Sea, we would drop buckets on a line to pick up the weed which was full of small beautiful crustaceans, plankton and also Portuguese Men O' War, quite beautiful too and weird but with a vicious sting for the unwary. On one voyage, going south we passed quite close to the rocky islands of Fenando de Noronha rising steeply from the ocean and which are about two hundred miles off the bulge of Brazil. A few natives were fishing from log rafts quite some way out. I remember being quite surprised that anyone lived there. Now they are a tourist resort and World Heritage location!

Later, when I became involved with the navigation, I learned that the wartime practice was that only the last known position was left on the chart and all others were expunged. Likewise no records of the navigational calculations were kept. It was not until the war was over that I was able to keep a proper sight book.

When well out in the ocean we had our first practice shoot at a floating target that Chippy had made for the occasion and which was dropped overboard. After it had fallen about two miles astern we altered course and the Second Mate called out the range and deflection. I repeated it, adjusted my wheels and called "Sights set." The layer and trainer called that they were "On", the Second Mate shouted "Fire!" and two feet in front of my nose with a flash of flame, a blast of hot air and a leap of recoil there was the most almighty bang I had ever heard in my life. I had no earplugs as I had to be able to hear the sight corrections called out by the Second Mate. No wonder I'm now deaf!

The whole crew had turned out on deck to see how good we were. We fired four rounds and didn't hit the target, but everyone agreed that if it had been a sub then they would have been worried—so would we have been!

The twelve-pounder AA gun was different and went off with more of a crack. There was no sight setting to do on that gun which had open ring sights and I became fuse setter, usually at 750 yards, and a member of the supply party.

On entering neutral ports Joe had to withdraw the firing pins of his guns and they were sealed into 'bond'. He could not wear his RN uniform ashore, but that didn't worry Joe, he was only there for the beer.

Now that we no longer called at the Canaries or the Azores, the much longer passage meant that we had a longer period on 'hard tack' and limejuice. More inconvenient in a personal way was the limited supply of fresh water and for the last couple of weeks we would be limited to a bucket per day per man with the pump locked at night-time. As we usually didn't get dirty when on passage this was no hardship: the problem was washing clothes—but we had a technique.

Our bathroom had a full length white enamelled cast iron bath but the only tap gave out cold salt sea water, so we placed a board across the top of the bath on which stood our bucket of warm fresh water from the galley supply. One washed down or bathed standing up, a technique which we called a 'Western Ocean'. When performing these ablutions, one put all the clothes one was wearing (which after all, in the tropics was probably only pants, vest and shorts) into the bottom of the bath and trod on them whilst bathing. One rinsed them out in the water remaining in the bucket—two jobs done in one.

In home waters it was not so simple. During wartime when ashore we used our number one uniform much more often and the vulnerable parts were the cuffs and collar of the white cotton shirts which soon got dirty. Whilst the officers were wealthy enough to have a good supply of shirts and to pay to have them laundered, we 'poor' apprentices had just two or three and had to launder our own. That was not too difficult, the problem was to make them look presentable—no 'drip dry' non-iron in those days and no electric iron. We did our best by 'ironing' just the front part of the shirt and the cuffs with the flat part of a Gordon's gin bottle, into which near boiling water had been poured. The collars, which of course were detached, were easier and more successful to do. First clean the mirror, then smooth out the damp collar and rub it onto the glass, best side to. It sticks there and when dry can be peeled off ready to wear.

Another innovation which showed that slowly we were getting organised was that we had a Zigzag Book in which was printed, illustrated and numbered various zigzag patterns about a mean course for a period of one or two hours. The amount of alteration and time on each course was irregular so that it was unpredictable to an observer—such as a U-boat. There were areas of ocean where we were advised to zigzag. Then the courses for the helmsman to steer and the times of alteration were chalked on a board that was placed in front of him, together with an old alarm clock, since the zigzag time varied from the ship's time.

We still had the old gent previously mentioned as Third Mate. It was his habit when on watch, as with all the other officers, to walk more or less continuously from one side of the bridge to the other, so keeping a lookout all round. One day some joker secretly wound up the alarm and set it to go off at eleven o'clock at night. Imagine a dark night, all quiet, no lights, a bit of tension maybe because of hidden dangers and just as the old gent passed the binnacle the alarm went off! I was told he nearly jumped out of his skin and so irate was he that he threw the still ringing alarm clock overboard. Later a proper clock was installed which could be programmed to give a ping as each alteration of course was due.

I see from my indentures that this return voyage took only a little over four months so it must have been uneventful. We went to Weymouth, wondering why, and found the bay to be full of merchant shipping. It must have been early May 1940.

A small naval party came aboard next day and we learned about magnetic mines and 'degaussing'. The magnetic mine was an early and very successful German 'secret weapon', in some months sinking as many merchant ships as the U-boats. In November 1939 when the tide was out two of them were observed to be on the mud-flats off Dungeness. A very brave RN officer dismantled them, 'volunteers' recovered them, their secret was out and counter measures put into effect.

One of them was called degaussing. During manufacture the constant hammering would cause a ship's hull to acquire its own magnetic field (if you think of the old school physics demonstration of putting a steel bar in the line of the Earth's magnetic field and then hammering it you will know what I mean). The degaussing countermeasure was to pass electric cables around the perimeter of the ship which when electrified would neutralise the permanent magnetism built into the ship's hull.

Another naval party came off the next day in a drifter and laid what appeared to be miles of black insulated cable in the scuppers around the ship and tied it off to the stanchions. At the same time the Chief Engineer was pacing the deck and sounding off to anybody who would listen what a preposterous idea the whole thing was and that 'his' generator couldn't possibly stand the extra load and would almost certainly blow up. It didn't.

Then we had to pass over the Degaussing Range to be tested and tuned and finally, since the ship's magnetism had changed, so had the compass deviation and the compasses had to be 'swung' and adjusted. In the binnacle below were many long bar magnets arranged in racks and which the professional adjuster would move to the optimum position for various ship headings. There were also two large soft iron balls, one on either side of the compass bowl and vertically on the fore side was a large cylindrical magnet in a case, called rather romantically I thought, 'Flinder's Bar'. What they all did I can't remember now but there were jingles to aid memory, one of which referred to ships with red noses and blue arses.

The compass error varied all the time of course according to what cargo we carried, what direction we were heading and where in the world we were. It was one of the duties of the officer of the watch to calculate from our known position the true bearing of the sun and compare it with the compass bearing, so establishing its error, which was recorded in the 'Compass Error Book'. This could be done much more easily by using the Pole Star.

We left Weymouth and headed for Hull. On the way up the

Humber we were told to put in our requests for a sub and as I knew I would be going on leave I asked for ten pounds. By the time the Old Man was back and ready to issue the money it was dark. Louis, Joe and I had decided we would walk to the nearest pub for a swift half. I followed Joe who had a torch along the cluttered deck to the saloon where the money was being issued.

On emerging from the bright saloon it was pitch dark outside but knowing my way around the ship I thought the best thing to do was to walk in the direction of the ship's rail and follow it along. I walked right over the side of the ship and fell on to the barge along-side! During the afternoon we had been discharging into the barge and our handrail had not been replaced.

I had fallen about fourteen feet I suppose, but I dared not move about much because I didn't know where the edge of the barge was and I didn't want to fall off into the dock—I still had my ten pound note in my hand! I couldn't think how to get back aboard, but I knew Joe was next in the queue behind me and I should hear his boots as he walked along the steel deck, so I waited. Sure enough it wasn't long before I heard them, so I called out "Joe!" The walking stopped. I called again and he said "Where are you?" I said "I'm on the barge over the side". He came to the ship's side and shone his torch down on to me, saying "What are you doing down there you silly bugger? Hang on, I'll get a rope ladder." He had to get help and by the time the ladder arrived the news had got around. The Old Man arrived too. He was very concerned; I was shepherded into the now deserted saloon and given the traditional but medically wrong treatment for shock—half a glass of brandy. It was difficult to be-lieve that I had suffered no ill effects, but it was true and after dust-ing off my great coat we went for that first beer. Someone would have got a wigging for that mishap.

I was able to take some leave. Father had received from the ship-ping company my marked first year examination papers with a note from the Examination Board drawing attention to the high marks that I had achieved. Everyone was pleased. I felt that I was on my way.

On returning to the St. Merriel at the start of my fifth voyage I found that the temporary degaussing had been replaced by a permanent installation around the perimeter of the 'tween decks with a control panel on the bridge.

Slowly over time the composition of the crew changed. Many of the East European seamen were still with us, but a few had left and were replaced by Yorkshiremen or Welshmen. We had a new Bosun, a Swede, one of the trilby hat brigade with a creased face and probably not as old as he looked. He was a fine seaman and always called me 'Al'—to rhyme with pal. We got on well together.

Sadly, Captain Owens went too and was replaced by a very smart but rather aloof figure whose name I cannot remember. During the voyage that followed I had the temerity to ask to see him and complained that the food we were getting at second sitting in our mess was not of the quality that was going into the officers' dining saloon, which it should have been. He received me courteously and dismissed me with no comment but he put the matter right and I think I did my reputation a bit of good.

It was back to South Wales for coal and this was the last time we were to use the English Channel. According to the dates in my indentures the voyage changeover date was June 4th 1940, so we must have passed through shortly before the Dunkirk evacuation. I have to say I only vaguely remember that event. It was a terribly dark time. During the month of July the Luftwaffe began in earnest its attacks on the Channel shipping. On the eighteenth they even sank the Goodwin Lightship! I believe this was all part of or the beginning of the 'Battle of Britain'. German aircraft laid mines in the Thames and Welsh coastal waters.

We continued on to Swansea for another few thousand tons of Welsh coal. The centre of the town had been bombed right out and was just a tidy area of rubble. We found a pub called the Vale of Neath within walking distance of our berth and that was the limit of our social life.

I remember nothing more of the next voyage until we got to Freetown on the return leg, except that in some place I was rather astonished to receive a letter from Muriel Lear at Malvern School, to which I replied. A more onerous correspondence was dumped on Rogers and myself by the Old Man. There was an organisation called 'The Ship Adoption Society'. A class in some junior school would 'adopt' a ship, every child in the class would write a letter and the whole lot was sent off addressed to the Captain who then passed them on to us to answer. I must say it was a bit of a chore, especially as we couldn't say what we were doing or where we were, which I suppose is what they were interested in. When communications got long delayed this task fortunately for us fizzled out.

The German possession and use of the French Biscay ports greatly facilitated the marauding of both U-boats and raiders. By the end of November the following year they had sunk eighty-eight ships. Two of the raiders were caught and sunk. Between the end of March and July 9th 1940 six German surface raiders put to sea. These were the Atlantis, Thor, Widder, Orion and Kormoran, with our future ally the USSR providing two icebreakers to escort the Komet, disguised as a Russian freighter, across the waters north of Siberia to its East Asian operations.

In the Autumn of 1940 the Admiral Scheer sailed and sank eighteen ships. The Scharnhorst, Gneisenau and Admiral Hipper were all out raiding at various times. In South American ports we could see German merchant ships moored alongside and naively assumed that they couldn't get back to Germany because of our naval blockade. It's more likely that they were supply ships for their raiders.

A piece of good fortune that came out of the failed Norwegian campaign was that over one thousand Scandinavian ships came over to our side including some two hundred modern tankers which were administered by Norstraship in London. We met one of them in the North Sea.

By this time the southern approaches to the Irish Sea (Celtic Sea or St. George's Channel, call it what you will) had, like the English Channel, been mined by the Royal Navy so on the return leg we had to head north around the coast of Ireland to Oban for orders, and so began my first acquaintance with the west coast of Scotland. We left there in convoy through the Sound of Mull and turned right— what a marvellous view of the Highlands and Islands! On later occasions we went to Gairloch and then later again to Loch Ewe to join up with coastal convoys going round to the East Coast.

It was head north through The Minches, around Cape Wrath and along the north coast, through the Pentland Firth and south to Methil in the Firth of Forth. There we waited for the next convoy south. If the weather was fine and clear, these convoys could be delightful until within range of the German bombers or E-boats. In fog and poor visibility they could be terrible, the strain on the Old Man and officers must have been intense. There were all classes of ships in them from cargo liners and big tankers down to small coasters and flat irons—a most appropriate name given to the east coast colliers which looked like a flat barge with a bridge and funnel stuck on right aft.

We had to keep to the inside of the off shore mine fields and so the convoys were restricted to only two columns in width. If there were say forty ships, the theoretical length of the convoy at two cable lengths between ships was almost four miles. In reality the distance between ships could be anything from that to half a mile. Sometimes, if a ship was anywhere near the centre, it would be impossible to see the front and rear ends of the column.

You can imagine what happens: a dark night, the weather thickens, a ship up front thinks it's going to lose sight of the one ahead so increases speed. Everyone behind sees the ship ahead disappearing so takes the same action and soon everyone is belting along to catch up. Then the one in front suddenly sees the ship ahead out of the murk, realises it might over run, reduces speed and the same happens all down the line with ships over running each other and bunching, the whole process perhaps taking a couple of hours or more. At the same time you are on the alert for signals, rogue ships and even the enemy.

In the early days we used to pick up a RN gunner at Methil, equipped with a stripped Lewis gun, who stayed on the bridge until we got to our destination and was then transferred to another ship going back. We almost prayed for a Jerry bomber to come over so that he could have a go at it! We learned!

In the days of balloon barrages screening the cities, some bright spark had the idea of something similar for convoys, but instead of balloons we had kites. They were large cotton ones with bamboo frames, flown on a wire that went through a pulley at the foremast head and down to a hand winch. I don't remember ever having one that flew properly. We would get them up so far and then they would begin to oscillate and eventually gyrate so that they were looping the loop around the axis of the wire, usually carrying away the wireless aerial. Eventually one went into such an enormous circuit that it not only carried away the aerial but wound around the steam whistle lanyard as well, giving a very prolonged blast until we could turn off the steam. That was the end for the Old Man, we never flew one again.

Later we were supplied with real balloons, smaller than the land variety, and they were never any trouble. They were brought out to us at the west coast convoy port by boats manned by WRNS, (or where they ATS?) As they were the first British lasses we had seen in months they received a good welcome. The balloons were removed when we reached our destination, and then all was repeated in reverse when we left once again. They had the drawback that if the weather was thick, the balloons could be visible above the clouds to aircraft, even if the ships were hidden.

Hull was getting bombed regularly, sometimes severely, which knocked about its port facilities and at times we were sent instead on our return up the canal to Manchester, or I suppose I should say Salford. Wherever it was the routine was the same—off to the nearest telephone box as soon as possible to send a telegram, "Arrived safely letter follows". Neither my parents at home at Alvan, nor Edna, was on the telephone but one could dictate a telegram to the operator who would say how much money to put in the slot. For a penny a word the service worked very well.

I'm not certain of the exact chronology at this time but one trip round to Hull was more eventful than some others. Because of thick fog we could not get up the Humber and had to anchor off Spurn Point, with a lookout on the foc'stle head giving a long ring on the bell every minute as laid down by the Regulations for the Prevention of Collisions at Sea. It was a quiet Sunday morning but instead of the Old Man coming round on his inspection an AB hurried through the accommodation calling "Captain's orders, everybody aft! Everybody aft!" Everybody stopped what they were doing, which wasn't much, and complied, wondering what this strange order was all about.

It turned out that the lookout had spotted a mine drifting down on to us with the tide and the Old Man and the Mate had gone on to the foc'stle head to see if anything could be done. They thought it best that everyone else was out of the way. Nothing could be done. The mine slowly came up to our bow plating, gently bumped its way along the ship's starboard side and disappeared into the mist astern. It was one of those large horned variety that one used to see at the seaside made into a collection box for the lifeboats or ancient mariners and in theory it should have become safe when it broke from its mooring. One never knew.

From Hull I was given leave. Now that there was a war on in earnest there was no doubt that during the rest of my apprenticeship I would get leave each time we returned to the UK, the question was "How much?" Usually it was about a week, maybe a day or two longer. I just had to wait for a telegram recalling me to the ship.

Now that Edna and I were getting to know each other better our relationship became stronger and firmer and leave was something to look forward to as never before. It was probably on this leave that she took me up to Bentley to see some of her friends or it might be more true to say for some of her friends to see me. Bentley is to the north of Darlaston on a slightly higher elevation than its surroundings and as we walked home in the darkness we could see in the distance a red glow in the sky—the reflection on the clouds caused by that night's bombing raid on Birmingham. It made us realise that although we were young and looking to the future the prospects were rather uncertain.

7

CONVOY WILL SCATTER

A long way home from Freetown

On returning from leave to Hull I found the place was in a dreadful mess. There had been another severe air raid and a fair amount of damage had been done to the docks. A landmine had caught on a crane and exploded not far from the ship, leaving bits of angle iron and railway track scattered around, but no one on board had been hurt and the ship was undamaged.

I went on a two-day gunnery course which I thought had a very ingenious piece of equipment called The Dome (not of the Greenwich variety). It was a large hemisphere coloured white inside, maybe held up by air pressure and at its centre was a cine-projector with sound effects and a pretend machine gun. The RN petty officer instructor could project on to the underside of the dome cine-film of German aeroplanes attacking in level flight or dive bombing our 'position'. Using the ring sights of our pretend gun we fired at the attacker using what we hoped was the correct amount of aim off. The P O could see where our shots were going and gave advice. I thought it most useful.

Sailing from there in December 1940 on our next trip (my sixth on board the St. Merriel) would mean it was all the way back round the north of Scotland and down the Irish Sea to the Bristol Channel for some more Welsh coal. The shortage of shipping capacity was not only due to ships being lost but everything now took so much longer. The trip round from Hull to the Bristol Channel might involve us in three separate convoys—from Hull to Methil, from Methil to Loch Ewe and from Loch Ewe to South Wales.

There was a shortage of seamen too. During the depression of the thirties very much shipping had been laid up and seamen who had lost their jobs had to 'go ashore' and find a living the best they could. Many who had done that successfully were unwilling to return to the sea life with the poor wages then being paid. If I remember correctly an AB's wage was just about ten pounds monthly. I think a First Mate's pay was less than twenty-five pounds (he was the Chief Officer of the ship remember, second in command!) and there were no extras like marriage allowance, everything had to be paid for except food. The saying was that as long as young lads were willing to go to sea for nothing except the adventure the wages would never amount to much.

The Government had to find an answer. One was the 'Direction of Labour' directive, another was to increase pay to encourage people back and to do this they introduced a 'War Bonus'. It was not all that popular. The men said, "Why not put up the wages instead?" They thought the answer to that was that when the war ended the War Bonus would stop too, whereas a reduction in wages would have to be negotiated. The bonus paid was five pounds monthly to those under eighteen and ten pounds to those over eighteen with two years sea time. We apprentices were not particularly concerned with the arguments; more immediate to me was that the money I received was going up from one pound monthly (second year pay) to six pounds, real wealth! I would now be able to buy presents. I could walk along to the Scandinavian Bar on the Santos waterfront and buy my friends a drink! Later, when the bonus became ten pounds and my real pay also increased I actually began to save money and could see that I would be able to finance myself. As the saying goes, "It's an ill wind."

When I returned to the Saint Merriel I found that Captain Owens had returned too. I at least was very pleased. The galley wireless put out that he had been offered one of the new ships but had asked to go back to the old Merryhell. During the past trip I'd had the honour of serving on board this ship longer than anyone else had but I didn't mind giving way to Captain Owens. One result of this was that I was given better accommodation. I had not known that there was a spare cabin in the Engineers Quarters—provision for an extra junior engineer which we didn't carry. I could recall that when I first joined the ship the engineers weren't very happy that we two 'deck apprentices' were using their messroom. Now I was being invited to live in their accommodation and have the benefit of their steward!

Joe the Gunner was taken from us to be replaced by three 'hostilities only' ratings—Joe would have appreciated that! The 'old gent' of a Third Mate went and in his place came a young newly qualified fellow named Arthur Clayton who was to become a great friend. A new First Mate arrived; a smallish well-built Welshman named Ellis, quietly spoken, very competent and as tough as old boots. He did a thorough job himself and expected everyone else to do the same, especially us two apprentices whom he took very much under his wing. As the senior I was put on his watch. He made good use of me but he was very fair.

The war at sea was not going very well for us but we were getting better organised. The St. Merriel now had four plastic armoured anti-aircraft machine gun positions. Large wooden rafts were fitted to the shrouds with quick release gear and the water and emergency rations were accessible whichever way up the raft floated. Lifejackets made of kapok were much more convenient and comfortable and less likely to break one's neck than the old solid cork block ones. They were equipped with a whistle and a battery powered red light.

Lifeboats now had much better provisions and equipment, one of them being provided with a wind up, hand operated emergency wireless transmitter for sending an SOS. The problem on the Merriel was the boats themselves, which were clinker built of wood and in the tropics the planking shrank so much that they leaked like sieves. The only thing we could do was to lower them into the water at every opportunity. They usually sank until they were floating on their buoyancy tanks but the planks soon tightened up as the wood swelled. Fortunately, by then they were fitted with semi-rotary bilge pumps so it was part of the 'drill' to pump them out. At sea they were kept swung out between davits and bowsed against a long padded spar with a quick release slip so that they could be quickly lowered. Unfortunately this also left them exposed to the blast from a torpedo.

As we were sailing back up the North Sea, I had completed my evening watch and was fast asleep when Rogers burst into the cabin exclaiming, "Come on, wake up, everybody on deck! We've been in collision and the ship may be sinking!" Always prone to dramatics, one took what Rogers said with a pinch of salt. Nevertheless, it was clear that the engines had stopped so I dressed hurriedly and went on deck. Going north we had met head on in the darkness another convoy going south—no lights of course, and no moon—and had indeed struck a glancing blow on a Norwegian tanker. It could have been calamitous. We had a hole in our foc'stle plating through which part of the Norwegian's lifeboat, mast and oars had been projected. The AB's accommodation was a shambles but marvellously no one had even been hurt, and the hole was above the waterline!

We were able to steam slowly ahead and in the morning came orders to go to Dundee for repairs. We were there for about a week. Louis and I found that the town had an ice skating rink so we organised a group visit. We were able to hire boots and skates and ventured out on to the rink with hilarious consequences. There were those who were proficient, those who had never been on skates before and those like myself who fell (literally) between the two. The star of the outing was the 'old' Swedish Bosun who hadn't been on skates for years but who skated serenely round the rink with his hands behind his back and a very superior grin on his face

One accidental encounter had brought me into contact with a pretty young lassie named Winnie Bell. I saw her home, whereupon she asked me to write and gave me her address. We sailed unexpectedly next day on the evening tide when I was supposed to see her again.

By that time I was eighteen and a half and more importantly had two years sea time and so qualified for the ten pounds per month War Bonus. My pay doubled again—riches indeed. The new mate told me that in foreign ports he wanted Rogers and myself to keep a continuous twenty four hour shipboard watch between us—to keep an eye on things, the ship, cargo, moorings, stevedores, visitors, and when cargo was being worked to service the winches. He didn't mind how we did it as long as one of us was there and visible. It meant that we couldn't go ashore together but that didn't worry us. In the end we settled down to an eight hours on and eight hours off routine, changing at six in the morning, two in the afternoon and ten o'clock at night, relieving each other for meals. It meant that one had the opportunity for a half-day trip ashore or a swift half in the evening on alternate days, with now and then an uninterrupted sleep. When we separated from the outward convoy on route again for South America I sat the second year examinations.

As I've mentioned before there was a Seamen's Mission at Santos with a conscientious young Padre. I saw him aboard just after we arrived and directed him to the see the Mate. Not long afterwards he came to see me and said he had explained to the Mate that there were a number of resident Britons ashore who had organised themselves into a football team. They had a pitch and kit but wanted someone to play against—would we oblige? The Mate had promptly replied "Yes, go and see Hall, he'll fix it." Since this was an order, even though second hand, I said I'd try my best. It perhaps sounds boastful, but I think it shows the rapport I had with the 'lower deck' that it was not as difficult as I feared.

In retrospect my task was made simpler because the make up of our crew had changed. There was no longer a deep sea fishing fleet since the trawlers had been taken over by the navy. Their crews were probably given the choice of going into the Navy or joining 'our lot'. Not wishing to be subject to the discipline of the RN, some of the younger bloods came over to us. It was the first time some of them had been on long 'deep sea' voyages, but they were good seamen and when they had got used to our different tackle and routine they fitted in well.

Our Eastern European seamen had gradually left us and in Hull we picked up a fair number of those ex-fishermen. They found it hard to be away from home for four or five months at a time when they were used to fourteen-day trips, but they were willing to have a go at anything, including senoritas and football. We also had two or three Newfoundlanders but they were older, more sober and God fearing types.

To be fair to the Mate, who was one of the first I asked to play, he did so and turned out to be one of our better players. Nevertheless, he insisted that I should be captain. As with the ice skating, it turned out that we had a wide range of abilities, starting with the New Zealand sparks who was a rugby forward but who had never played soccer in his life—where ever the ball went he ran after it and once leaped high in the air and caught it!

Since we were in the heat of the tropics, the match started at eight o'clock in the evening on a floodlit pitch, long before we had them in England. I had to organise a taxi to collect a few freewheeling ABs and firemen from the Scandinavian Bar where they had gone for a 'livener' and Dutch courage. We had all thought we were pretty fit but everyone found thirty-five minutes each way to be very hard going. More than one, having made a dashing run, would retire to the sideline ditch for a minute or two to relieve themselves of their Dutch courage; by half time we had got our second wind. We never won a match—there were to be others as each time we arrived in Santos the Padre was waiting—but we had some grand celebrations at the Scandinavian Bar.

On one voyage we had a Hungarian steward with an unpronounceable name but who was known as Joe. He looked a bit like Manuel in Fawlty Towers. He didn't play football but one night it was discovered that he used to play the violin in a cafe orchestra. The 'Scan' had an ensemble of piano, drums, trumpet and violin. It was not long before the more vociferous and insistent members of the group had persuaded Joe to play and more remarkably the resident fiddler allowed Joe to use his violin. We had spirited renderings of The Blue Danube and other Viennese waltzes.

It occurs to me that by then there were no longer any 'boy' ratings in the crew: those deck boys and cabin boys etc. Older young 'assistant' stewards, cooks, deckhands and so on had replaced them. Perhaps young boys were no longer allowed to sign on as crew because of the war, but even so there were still sixteen year old cadet and apprentice deck officers!

Passenger liners had by now been converted into troopships or hospital ships and as such did not need the many stewards they had had previously. Some retrained in other departments while others descended the social scale to join the cargo ships, one of whom came to us, a very dapper little Scot who was of course known as Jock. He claimed to have a certain system for winning at Roulette that sounded feasible.

The spinner has thirty-eight holes numbered from one to thirty six plus two zeros. One can bet at odds of two to one on the 'dozens', which are one to twelve, thirteen to twenty-four and twenty-five to thirty-six, the two zeros being losing numbers. Jock's theory was that sooner or later the ball would fall into the same dozen two spins running—paying out at two to one—so if one followed the ball and increased one's stake each time to cover losses and make a profit (not necessarily doubling up each time), one could not but win.

It sounded like a reasonable system, so four of us made up a syndicate to play the casinos down the Brazilian coast at Santos, Rio and Rio Grande. Every time we made enough to cover our night out. Then we got to Buenos Aires and failure! I can remember that Jock, who had been placing the bets, left the table and walked over to us looking very serious. He explained that he had reached our limit—eight bets in succession had gone down. He felt one more bet would do it. It had never failed before—could he place one more bet? We agreed and we lost! Although a bit sad, we were not distressed, as we had had a good run for our money and overall we had done quite well. Jock left at the end of that trip and that was the end of the syndicate, which was perhaps as well!

The type of cargoes we loaded in South America changed at this time. At home the 'Min. of Ag.' had taken control of farm production and much acreage of grassland, heath and common had been put under the plough for cereal and root crops. Consequently shipping was freed from carrying these imports and other more necessitous goods were carried in their stead. From Brazil, we brought cotton bales and sugar that made the ship smell like a brewery. From the Argentine we carried hides, both wet and dry, which stank awfully, and tons and tons of corned beef—we must have fed the Eighth Army! We once carried some corned pork, which I thought delicious but have not seen or heard of since. We still carried cargoes of corn maize that I suppose we did not then grow in the UK.

We once carried a small deck cargo of logs from one of the Brazilian ports. I remember them being about eight feet long—dark, smooth and very heavy. They were also quite slippery. One of them escaped from its sling and plunged between the quay and the ship's side. When we looked into the gap the log had sunk! I asked the stevedores what it was but they could only call it 'Jungle Wood'. I think it must have been Rosewood or Lignum Vitae.

How long we stayed in one port depended of course on the kind of cargo we were working and how much of it there was. Bulk maize we could load in a couple of days or so but probably the average stay was for about ten days.

On one occasion (fortunately only once) we loaded a full cargo of chrome or manganese ore at one of the north Brazilian ports, although 'full' is something of a misnomer since that means enough to take us down to our marks, about 9000 tons. It was very dense, heavy stuff and I remember looking into the holds and seeing a small heap of reddish orange crumbly material in each one. I think we loaded some cotton bales in the 'tween decks to raise the centre of gravity, but even so, once we got into the South Atlantic swells, with all that bottom weight we rolled swiftly, energetically and not at all comfortably. No one said much, but I'm sure most people were thinking as I was, that if we get torpedoed with this lot on board the old ship will break up and go down like a stone. We got back safely though and it must have been on this trip that we were directed round the north of Scotland to Middlesborough, which had a very grim dockland indeed and from where I was able to go on leave.

Then there was the voyage with the bananas. Whose idea it was

I don't know but at one of the Brazilian ports we loaded a cargo of bananas on the fore and after decks to take to Buenos Aires. The stalks, quite green, were stacked about six feet high. This was quite a novelty at first and probably everybody had a hand or even a whole stalk hanging somewhere for private consumption. Alas, either the fruit was not green enough, the weather was hotter than expected, or the voyage took longer than calculated for when we got to BA they were too ripe and the consignee wouldn't take them. Whilst the agent tried to find another buyer the whole lot went rotten. Gradually, the six-foot high stacks became eighteen inches of black stinking mush and the dockers said they wouldn't touch it. The smell was awful. Eventually a soap factory said it would have them. Barges were brought alongside and the crew had to offload the rotting bananas into them. It took us two days. We started off wearing long seaboots and tried to be careful but it was no use, the sticky filth just worked its way up and into everywhere. Eventually we found the best way was to work as nearly naked as possible, throwing away the little clothing we had worn. I've not eaten a banana since.

Our Chief Steward was able to buy tinned butter from the ship's chandlers, which he then sold on to us and of course it was a good present to take home, as was sugar which was also tightly rationed.

For girl friends we obtained silk stockings that were the cause of much mirth on purchase. The technique was to go into a store or a haberdasher and explain by mime and dockside Spanish or Portuguese what we wanted. Of course the question always was, 'What size?' The only way to answer that was to find a young lady assistant of the appropriate dimensions and say 'Like this one'.

Edna's father was a pipe smoker who 'liked a bit of twist'—which was not always appreciated by his wife and daughter! If I took him a 'plug' or two of ship's tobacco his face would light up with appreciation. I could have his daughter!

In March 1941 we left Freetown in a homeward convoy, code number SL68. So far the war at sea had not produced anything startling for us. We had been bombed one evening during an East Coast convoy and on many occasions we had seen and heard escorts depth charging, but whether they had been real or merely suspected submarines we didn't know. This time we had what seemed like a reasonable escort, certainly more impressive than we had had before, comprising a couple of destroyers and two or three corvettes. I have only admiration for the men who served on those sturdy little tubs, they must have been thrown around all over the place, but what we didn't know was that a sub on the surface could outrun them. We were about to find out.

When the convoy sailed we were number thirty two—the second ship in the third column—a position we were happy with since nobody liked to be on the outside, unless they were one of the few masters who didn't like close neighbours. The WW1 battleship HMS Malaya had taken station in the middle of the convoy.

All went well for about three days. Towards the end of my evening watch I was keeping lookout on the port side of the bridge with the Mate to starboard on the Commodore's side. With a great roar and two orange flashes, two ships were torpedoed on our port side, to be followed soon after by a third towards the convoy centre. Captain Owens was on the bridge immediately. To me, who had seen nothing like it before, it was quite terrifying—so unexpected. We had naively thought that the darkness was our friend, hiding us from the enemy. We had not heard of the submarines' new tactic of lying in wait ahead of the convoy and then attacking hull down on the surface, taking advantage of their low silhouette to be virtually invisible in the darkness and their superior speed to withdraw. The rest of the night was quiet but uneasy.

When dawn broke we could see the Malaya was 'down by the head' and made jocular remarks that she must have been torpedoed. It was in fact true! During the day she probably repositioned ballast because she gradually regained a more even attitude.

Next day there seemed to be more signalling than usual between the escort and Commodore but we were not in position to read it. We wondered what the night would bring. It brought almost the same as before, more ships torpedoed at more or less the same hour but this time the escort fired off star shells to illuminate the scene and the offending U-boat(s). To those of us unused to such things it just made us feel more exposed. In my mind's eye now I still have a picture of a single corvette, looking very lonely in the pale silvery light, a couple of flares hanging in the darkness above.

There was yet a third night of attacks during which a Dutch freighter in our next starboard column 'caught a packet.' I heard the Old Man call out, 'There goes the Dutchman!' I can still see her with a tall pillar of orange flame going up vertically and the derricks and debris being hurled upwards; she seemed almost to stop in her tracks.

When dawn broke on our morning watch we were amazed and not all that pleased to find that we were leading the outside column with only three ships in it! The ship ahead and all nine ships in the two columns outside us had disappeared. There were gaps inside the convoy too. I don't think for a minute that all had been torpedoed, although some had of course. The war was by now just over eighteen months old and although it was proven statistically that ships were safer in convoy even if the escort was minimal—and during those early days it was rather thin—there were still masters who were prepared to chance it on their own. I think some of the ships had decided to clear off under cover of darkness. After all, it is said one can prove anything with statistics.

John Slader in his book 'The Red Duster at War' (Kimber, 1988) says that the battle cruisers Scharnhorst and Gneisenau sighted this convoy on March 7th, but having also seen the Malaya veered away on the misty horizon and called in the U-boats 124 and 105.

What Captain Owens thought I don't know but the decision was made for us. Some large alterations of course were made during the day and in the late afternoon the Commodore flew the signal 'Convoy will scatter at so and so hours', which was at dusk. There was an orderly way of doing this so that the convoy opened out like a fan and after a given time ships settled on their allotted courses. This we did and as far as we were concerned we got away with it. How the other ships fared I don't know. It was just as well that we didn't know the Germans had broken our Admiralty Convoy Code!

We received radio instructions to proceed to Bermuda across the other side of the Atlantic! We didn't have a chart but the Second

Mate got the latitude and longitude from an atlas and that was good enough. From there we were sent to St. John's in Newfoundland and thence joined a transatlantic convoy back to the UK.

On return I was able to take leave in late May or early June. Edna had time off work so we borrowed a couple of bicycles and made trips out into the local countryside, one of them to Sutton Park. There was at that time a cultivated area but much of it was open grassland, fairly high up and with good views. We put down the bikes and rested on the grass. Edna opened her handbag—this may have been engineered—and I caught sight of one or more of my letters. Out of curiosity I asked to see them. I've mentioned before the difficulty of writing letters when the important things are censored and I just wanted to see how my efforts had turned out. She seemed reluctant at first, saying something like, "You'll kick yourself if you do", which of course only made me more curious. Eventually she handed over a letter and I began to read. It seemed all right at first but as I went from sheet one to sheet two they didn't seem to run together. I was puzzled but I soon saw what I had done.

It was my habit when on a voyage to write a number of letters at the same time so that when we got to port they were all ready to go. I had done this on the previous trip after I had met Winnie Bell and promised to write. I kept my promise but had included with Edna's letter the middle page of Winnie's! Then I had a pang of conscience that I shouldn't be doing this to Edna and had thrown away, as I thought, the letter to Winnie. What an embarrassment! As I realised what I had done I saw what I thought was a comic side and began to laugh. My dear Edna pointed out to me that this was no laughing matter for her.

I have to admit that it became clear to me that she had been treating our affair much more seriously than I had. She had been visiting my parents each week whilst I was away and rather than upset them by 'breaking it off' she had decided to wait and confront me. I explained what had happened and that I had never sent the other letter anyway. I think she believed me. This had great personal significance because I realised how important Edna was to me and that I must not jeopardise our relationship again.

1. *This is the document that bound me to the B & S Shipping Company for four years. There was some 'elasticity'. I did receive laundered bed linen but not the 12 shillings for washing and because of the war I was released six months early but did not receive the £5.*

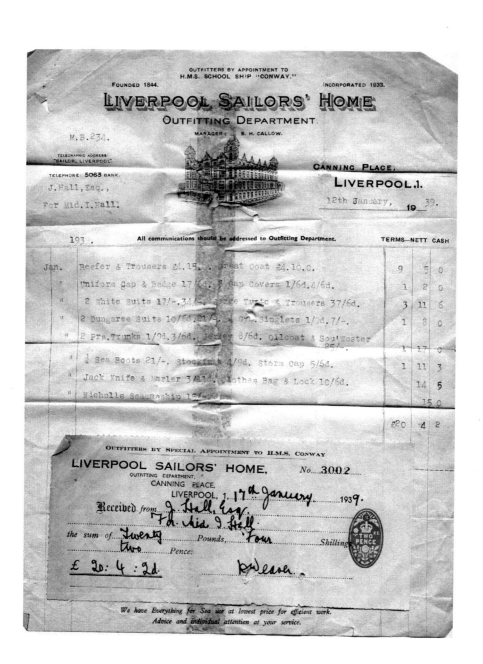

OUTFITTERS BY APPOINTMENT TO
H.M.S. SCHOOL SHIP "CONWAY."

FOUNDED 1844.   INCORPORATED 1933.

LIVERPOOL SAILORS' HOME
OUTFITTING DEPARTMENT.

MANAGER: B. H. CALLOW.

M.B.234.

TELEGRAPHIC ADDRESS:
"SAILOR, LIVERPOOL".

TELEPHONE: 5063 BANK.

J.Hall, Esq.,

For Mid.I.Hall

CANNING PLACE,
LIVERPOOL.1.

12th January, 19 39.

193 .   All communications should be addressed to Outfitting Department.   TERMS—NETT CASH

Jan.	Reefer & Trousers £4.15... Great Coat £4.10.0.	9	5	0
"	Uniform Cap & Badge 17/6d. 3 Cap Covers 1/6d.4/6d.	1	2	0
"	2 White Suits 17/-.34/-. Serge Tunic & Trousers 37/6d.	3	11	6
"	2 Dungaree Suits 10/6d.21/-. 4 Gym.Singlets 1/9d.7/-.	1	8	0
"	2 Prs.Trunks 1/9d.3/6d. Jersey 8/6d. Oilcoat & Sou'wester 25/-.	1	17	0
"	1 Sea Boots 21/-. Stockings 4/9d. Storm Cap 5/6d.	1	11	3
"	Jack Knife & Marler 3/4½d. Clothes Bag & Lock 10/6d.		14	5
"	Nicholls Seamanship 15/-.		15	0
		£20	4	2

OUTFITTERS BY SPECIAL APPOINTMENT TO H.M.S. CONWAY

LIVERPOOL SAILORS' HOME,   No. 3002
OUTFITTING DEPARTMENT,
CANNING PLACE,
LIVERPOOL, 1. 17th January 1939.

Received from J.Hall, Esq.
For Mid I Hall

the sum of Twenty Pounds, Four Shillings
two Pence:

£ 20 : 4 : 2d.   Weaver.

TWO PENCE

We have Everything for Sea use at lowest price for efficient work.
Advice and individual attention at your service.

2.   *Kit List.*

81

3. *All dressed up. Taken in the garden at home on the eve of my departure for the St.Merriel at Milwall docks.*

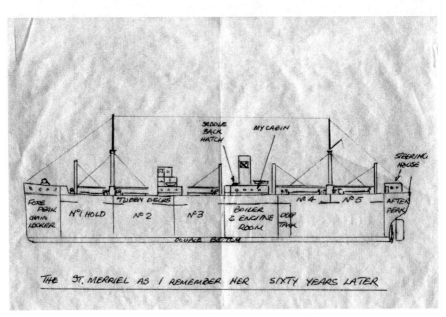

4. *Sketch of the Saint Merriel*

5. *Boys of the Cape Verde Islands who would dive for coins thrown into the sea. Pennies then were bigger than now!*

6. *Titch the Galley Boy from Hull. School leaving age 14, his voice not yet broken he had literally stepped from the classroom into the galley which he had just been scrubbing out.*

7.   *Boxing. Louis gives instruction in the noble art. His hair is not even ruffled.*

8.   *Milder weather brings dhobi day. Note the piece of Bosun's hard yellow soap.*

9.   Time off for some of the crew in Buenos Aries.

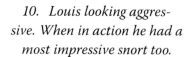

10. Louis looking aggressive. When in action he had a most impressive snort too.

11. *Filthy and fit. Rogers and I on the quayside at Santos. The ship's side is in the background..*

12. *This is the only convoy photograph I was able to take. Where we were I do not know.*

*13. Darts. If the dart missed the
board it hit the steel bulkhead!*

14. Reading the signals.

15. Ready for a 'Western Ocean' with the day's supply of hot water. Though of poor quality this is one of my favourite photographs. This is reality – nothing posed.

16. Stevedores breaking out the coal cargo. Santos.

17. On the quayside at BA. I cannot remember what the celebration was but it obviously indicates a happy ship.

18. 'Old Salt' – our much liked Swedish Bosun, with trilby hat!

19. The three hostilities only DEMS gunners who replaced Joe.

20. The 'Young Salt.'

21. *Discharging coal at Buenos Aires. Much steam escaping from badly maintained winches.*

22. *Discharging coal, afterdeck. On the port side derricks are plumbed over the quay. On the starboard side tubs are being hoisted on to the deck then craned off to a barge alongside.*

8

SOUTH AMERICA WAY

Shore leave with the Missionaries

Just before leaving home to return to the St. Merriel, I had asked Father to write to the Company to say that, if possible, I would like to be transferred to another ship before completing my indentured service in order to broaden my experience. Before we sailed on my seventh voyage I received a letter from Father to say that the company had written to him acknowledging this request. Enclosed, with their pleasure, was a Certificate that had been awarded to me by the Officers' Training Board for the high standard of work submitted to them in my second year examinations. I also received another letter from Muriel Lear to say that she was back in Buenos Aires and asking me to get in touch the next time I was there, when perhaps I could stay with her family for a day or so.

For a long time now convoys outward bound from the Bristol Channel had gone up the Irish Sea from Milford Haven and around the north of Ireland, shedding ships to and picking them up from other ports on the way. Thinking about it now, the organisation was superb. Off the north coast of Ireland our ocean escort came out from Londonderry to meet us and the coastal one departed. Some of the escorts began to appear with strange cage like constructions fixed to their masts or superstructure—the beginnings of radar and High Frequency direction finding equipment. Strange flying boats called Catalinas came out and patrolled round the convoys in addition to the beautiful old Sunderlands, and how glad we were to see them!

The signing on date for this voyage is given on the back of my Indentures as May 8th. 1941. On the 27th Of May the Bismark was sunk. We had already sailed when we heard the news so what we received was scanty. There was little rejoicing because the loss of our own Hood was too sobering. At this time Doenitz switched the U-boat attacks to the convoys off the West African coast, with thirty ships being sunk in May, but my time on the runs to South America was soon to end.

Before we sailed I had told our Swedish Bosun that I was a bit fed up with the four to eight watch after nearly two and a half years. I asked if he was prepared to have me on day work, and if so would he suggest the change to the Mate. He would and did and the Mate approved. I had always liked the manual work of a ship and I had a good experienced AB from Hull to work with, as well as all the others who appeared at various times throughout the day on their field days. What's more I had an undisturbed night's sleep and Saturday afternoon and Sunday off work. However, the Old Man was not going to let me disappear like that so easily. I was still sent for to take the helm on entering and leaving port and occasionally in bad weather, when we were hove to and he wanted someone at the wheel whom he knew.

Once we had cleared from the convoy and settled on the long trek south, the Old Man sent for me to congratulate me on my exam success. He said he was pleased that I was taking my studies seriously and he thought it was time that I did some practical navigation. Thus I should report to the bridge on Sunday morning and he would teach me to use a sextant and to find latitude at noon. To say that I was thrilled is an understatement.

'Noon Sights' was the event of the day when the ship's position was fixed by observation. It was the end of one working day and the beginning of the next. It was the Second Mate's responsibility really but most masters, and Captain Owens was such a man, took part and so did the Third Mate who was on watch anyway. So, on the appointed hour I turned up, Arthur the Third Mate welcomed me, the Second Mate looked a bit askance and the Old Man took me in hand. As he would know from looking at my exam papers, I could already do it in theory, what I lacked was the practical experience which he was able to provide. It was the cause of a bit of good natured ribbing by my lower deck friends when they saw me standing on the bridge beside the Old Man with one of his sextants.

Using 'Meridian altitude' is quite simple really and after a couple of weeks I was expected to go up on Sunday mornings after breakfast and take part in the longitude sights. This was when Arthur Clayton took me in hand. Capt. Owens used a rather old fashioned formula to calculate longitude, but Arthur used a different system called the 'Marc St. Hilaire Intercept Method', which he was keen to introduce to me and which I eventually adopted. From then on it became usual for me to spend Sunday mornings on the bridge taking sights, helping Arthur with his watch and getting used to the bridge routine. In convoy, it was the practice of the Commodore to hoist a signal at noon showing his observed position, and all ships followed suit showing their own calculations. It was rather like a sweep as to who would be nearest to the Commodore—not that he was likely to be more correct than anyone else was. The Second Mate slowly warmed to me.

During peacetime and when sailing unescorted we kept 'Sun Time'. Noon was when the sun was at it's highest altitude and traditionally the ship's clocks were timed so that twelve o'clock midday was five minutes later than observed noon, so that there was time to 'work up the position' before the midday meal. The ship's clocks were altered during the Mate's evening watch to accommodate the change in longitude. Going westwards the Second Mate would go up to the bridge at about a quarter to six and turn back the clock, say eight minutes, and tell the helmsman to ring Four Bells at four minutes to the hour, so splitting the time between the two halves of the watch. I remember what a cruel blow this was, having stood at the wheel for almost two hours and looking forward to being relieved, then to be told that I had to do a few minutes extra. Of course we got it all back going eastwards on the journey home.

When in convoy, however, all ships—naval and merchant—kept 'Zone Time' so that there was no doubt between us as to what time it was. This meant that usually there was a one hour alteration when passing from one time zone to the next and the hour would be shared out twenty minutes to each night time watch. To have to do twenty minutes extra was a terrible imposition—it seemed endless.

It must have been at about this time whilst we were on the South American coast that Arthur contracted some malady for which a shore doctor prescribed a course of injections. The syringe and ampoules were supplied in a neat, flat lidded box and were delivered into the custody of the Chief Steward, as keeper of the medicine chest. The injection had to be made into the muscles at the top back of the leg just below the cheek of his back-side. This ordeal took place at seven o'clock in an evening and for a short while was the entertainment of the day. Arthur had to lie face down on his bunk, backside exposed. All the mid-ship crowd who were not on duty gathered at the open door of his cabin to watch the performance and to offer much ribald advice as Jack the steward, with great theatrical flourishes, prepared his patient and finally plunged in the needle. Arthur put up with this for about four injections but it got too much for his self esteem—having found out where Jack kept the apparatus Arthur stole it and dumped it over the side. He still managed to recover!

I had yet another accident, so similar to the previous one as to be uncanny. At Santos we had lost another football match, finished discharging and had loaded cotton bales in some of the 'tween decks before commencing to move south to Buenos Aires. We left at dusk in very much of a hurry, battening down and lowering derricks as we went down river in the gathering darkness. I've guessed that this was to surprise enemy agents and get away well before they could report our departure.

As we broke out into the open sea there came a call from the bridge to get the wireless aerial rigged. I had never known such urgency before, but as the wire was hauled up to the mastheads it fouled something on the boat deck. Knowing my way around even in the darkness I called, "I'll do it" and shinned up the ladder by the galley. Taking the wire aerial in my right fist I intended to work my way along the boat deck until I came to the obstruction, took two or three strides and disappeared down the 'saddleback hatch'. This was a small hatch in front of the funnel where the coal had been loaded when the ship was a coal burner, the saddleback or metal shute splitting the coal delivery to either side. At the bottom the wings or 'tween decks were now blocked off with bales of cotton. Some of the hatch covers had been left off for ventilation and I had dropped through the gap.

Again I was in a situation where I couldn't do anything about it. If I climbed up to the top of the saddleback I couldn't reach the opening. I could only call out, "Help!" All was quiet and still. Trying to sound as though I was not in any great trouble I called "Help!" again whereupon I heard the Old Man call out in some urgency from the bridge, "It's Hall, he's fallen down the engine room!" There was a clatter of footsteps up the iron ladder as the rescue party mounted and I was able to call out, "It's all right, I'm in the saddleback." The Mate shone his torch, sent for a rope ladder and sent a message to the Old Man that all was well.

I climbed out unharmed except for friction burns and some skin missing from the palm of my hand where the wire had run through as I dropped. I was escorted into the saloon and given the usual treatment by the Chief Steward, this time half a glass of port and brandy. Whilst he was cleaning and dressing my 'wound', the Old Man came down his stairs to see for himself bringing his own contribution, another half glass of brandy and the instructions that I should go to bed and turn in. I did!

Owing to my new affluence of eleven pounds ten shillings per month, before we left Brazil I was able to fulfil my ambition and buy for Edna a crocodile skin handbag with a real small crocodile head affixed to it. These were highly thought of then, but like fur coats they are not nowadays to be seen in public. Fortunately I also bought a jewellery box veneered in South American woods which she still has on her dressing table today.

When we reached BA I did my usual job of hanging over the bows of the ship in a bosun's chair with two small brushes and two pots of paint, one white, the other black. I painted in the draught figures whist the ship was still high out of the water.

Somehow I was in touch with Muriel again—I think I received a letter. It would be no secret that the ship was there, for Argentina was a neutral country, albeit a pro nazi one. She asked me to find out if I could go and stay with them for a few days and if so she would come and fetch me. As it was obvious that we would be there for some time I asked to see the Old Man and explained the situation. He gave me an artful look and said he would have a word with the Mate, the outcome being I was given three days leave.

I rang Muriel, who told me she would meet me at some permanent fair ground place, which was quite famous but I can't remember the name now. Her two younger brothers were there too and after a couple of hours on the rides we caught the bus to where she lived at Quilmes, some distance out of the city. I was made very welcome.

With other young members of the local English residents group, we went horse riding. I'd never sat on a horse before, but then we went rowing at the riverside rowing club at which I was more proficient.

I remember the spaciousness of their bungalow, the excellent food (although there were no pink gins) and that there was domestic help. One of the rooms was a workshop with small printing presses but whether these were used to propagate the Gospel I don't know. At the back of my mind was the thought that these people are missionaries, being supported by the gifts and charity of working class people at home like my father and mother, who have nowhere near this standard of living and certainly can't afford to send their daughters to Malvern School.

It all seemed rather strange. Although Muriel was a nice looking lass, a natural blonde (blondes had scarcity value in those days before the advent of the L'Oreal and Garnier Laboratories) whom I liked very much, with an attractive and pleasant personality, I did not feel physically attracted to her. I was a bit concerned. I had escaped from religious influence once before and I didn't want to become embroiled again. Besides, I had a girl at home to whom I was attracted and committed. However, the problem, if there ever was one was solved for me. I never sailed to South America again.

When we got back to the UK I was told by the Company to pack my kit, to go on leave and to wait for instructions to join another ship. The St. Merriel had been a good home to me for two and three quarter years. I was to meet with her and Captain Owens once more.

After I had left the ship I realised that I had left my old 'Box Brownie' camera behind in the ship's bond. It seemed too difficult a task to try and recover it so that was the end of any personal photographs.

It is only since starting to write these reminiscences that I have realised how lucky I was to have served under such men as Captain Owens, Chief Officers Campbell and Ellis, and Third Officer Arthur Clayton, and how much I owed to them. It was from them that I learned at first hand the duties of a deck officer and that there is great personal satisfaction in doing one's duty to the best of one's ability.

I must not forget either, the three boatswains I have mentioned—the Hebridean, the Estonian and the Swede—who each in their own way took me under their care and made a seaman of me.

9

CHRISTMAS IN ARCHANGEL

The Saint Clears joins an Arctic convoy

At the end of about a week's leave I received notice to join the SS St. Clears lying at North Shields. I was quite pleased about this.

The driving force behind the Saint Line was a man called Street—the 'S' of the old B & S company—who had the brains and initiative that made the company tick. During the mid nineteen thirties under the government's rebuilding program old ships were bought up and then cashed in for scrap to fund the building of new ships for the company by Thomson of Sunderland. The first of these were the Saints Clears, Helena and Margaret to be followed later by the Saint Rosario and a few others built during the war. Whereas the hull design of the St. Merriel was very traditional (a few years ago when I saw Brunel's Great Britain I could see how one had derived from the other), the hull form of these later ships was of a tank-tested design for economical running. Its construction was based on the engineering principle of using high strength materials in the areas most subjected to stress in a seaway and of saving weight elsewhere. A lighter and more economical structure resulted.

The propulsion unit was new. Instead of the large thumping three cylinders of the St. Merriel, there were two small compound engines side by side, each having two cylinders and the exhausts of which went into a geared turbine. This was an economical unit but it had the drawback that the ship could only go astern on the compounds, so 'full astern' was not quite full astern and pilots had to be told so.

The lower deck crew was not housed under the foc'stle head but aft in the poop. Amidships was a single block of accommodation. On the bridge deck was the chart room and radio office. The boat deck below had the deck officers' cabins on the starboard side and to port were the sparks' and apprentices' cabins. On this build of ship we were accommodated as junior officers! Below at main deck level to port were the engineers' cabins and a mess room used by all the officers. Nearby was the galley and catering staff accommodation. Adjoining and forward of this was accommodation for twelve passengers and their dining and recreation room, and somewhere in amongst this was the Old Man, who had access to the bridge. Rising up between the officers' accommodation and that of the engineers and apprentices was the engine room trunking.

There were three holds forward and two aft. These ships were oil burners and had refrigerators—so no more salt beef, pork and fish! Although I was glad to be there for the experience, I realise that I never took to the St. Clears quite like I did to the St. Merriel. She seemed to be rather 'tinny' compared with the ruggedness of the latter.

Trade for the B & S Company had originally been to take coal out of South Wales ports to Canada and to bring grain back, but Street wanted to break into the South American passenger trade with Antwerp, which these ships enabled him to do. A regular sailing schedule was advertised which I think cost £65 return and the trip took a little over three months. A bachelor retired army officer took up a permanent berth on the St. Helena. He said it was more congenial and cheaper than living ashore and with duty free cigarettes, whisky and gin at five shillings a bottle he was probably correct.

The St. Clears seemed to be in pretty much the same state as the St. Merriel had been when I first joined her—crew paid off and discharged and not much happening. I dumped my kit in the apprentices' room that had bunks for four but I knew there would only be two of us so we would not be cramped. The door opened straight on to the boat deck so it would be a straightforward exit in times of emergency. Outside was our own w.c. and separate wash room, all very reasonable and on the same deck as the officers! It meant though that we did not have the same contact with the lower deck that we had had on the Merriel and I'm glad I didn't miss that in my early days.

When the North American built 'Liberty' ships first appeared I thought how similar they looked to these three sister ships. It was only very recently I learned that when the idea of the Liberty ships was being considered Thomson's chief designer was sent to the USA with his designs. They were accepted and adapted for mass production methods and to conform to the more generous US concept of crew accommodation.

Lo and behold, one of the first persons I came across was Barley, of whom I had not seen or heard since that first day on the St. Merriel. It turned out he had just got his Second Mate's ticket and this was to be his first ship as Third Mate. We had a few reminiscences about the Merriel and he told me the true story of the telegram and the bogus illness. He was still chuckling at the thought that he had dodged Tubby Campbell.

Dick Newman turned up from somewhere and introduced himself as the other apprentice. A month or two older than myself and about the same build, we became friends at once. Dick quite rapidly established that he was about two months senior to me, which seemed to please him, as I don't think he'd been senior apprentice before. As for myself I was quite pleased for it to be so, as I was looking forward to being on the eight to twelve watch away from the beck and call of the Mate.

Almost immediately we were told that the ship was to be fumigated and Dick and I were detailed to stay at an hotel in Whitley Bay for twenty-four hours. Whitley Bay in wartime November was no Riviera but it enabled Dick and I to get to know each other better. He was from Cheltenham, he had a sister who was a nurse and her friend was Dick's girl friend.

After the fumigation we went somewhere in the Tyne to load pithead waste as ballast in the bottoms of the holds, which was then levelled off and covered with dunnage boards. Barley, our Third Mate, promptly received a telegram calling him home for some emergency! It was common knowledge that to be ballasted as we were meant we would be loading military stores. I said nothing, but I reckoned Barley had put two and two together, decided we were going to Russia and chickened out.

Soon after, we received a replacement whose real name I cannot remember. Although he lived at Belper in Derbyshire, he had been born in Nova Scotia and still had the accent. Nova Scotians were known as 'Bluenoses' so our Third Mate was 'Bluey'. He too was newly ticketed. The Second Mate we didn't see much of and since Dick was senior to me he was the one who went to see the Mate to get our orders, so I didn't see much of the Mate either. On the St. Clears we didn't usually work with the seamen, but were given jobs to do on our own. I was having a quiet life after the Merriel.

We signed on a new crew, all Geordies of course. They turned out to be a grand lot, but it took Dick and I a couple of weeks to learn the language. We loaded the cargo at North Shields. Except for bombs, shells and ammo' which are heavy, military stores take up space but have not much weight, particularly transport such as trucks, vans, planes etc. Tanks have a bit more weight, but cannot be put on top of anything else and not much can be stacked on them—hence the ballast that was to provide some bottom weight and help to take us down to our marks. There was a twenty-five ton capacity 'jumbo' derrick on the foremast with which we could lift out the tanks we were taking, which I think were Valentines. I thought the two-pounder gun with which they were equipped looked rather puny.

All the vehicles had to be drained of petrol before they came aboard, which meant they had to be manhandled into their allotted space in the holds—more than one was manoeuvred in on its starter motor! Finally the deck cargo was put aboard, comprising mostly aircraft parts in crates but vehicles as well and lashed into place to cleats welded on to the deck. It was a new experience, both for us and for the military personnel who were responsible for the despatch and there was a fair amount of learning as we went along.

A meagre issue of 'hard weather' clothing was supplied: a type of duffel coat which will be mentioned later, and most usefully two pairs each of ribbed woollen 'long-johns'. The joke story was that on turning in one took them off and stood them in the corner. There was also one pair each of 'three finger, one finger, thumb' fur lined mittens. Before we sailed about half a dozen sacks of woollen 'comforts' came aboard which Dick and I were told to distribute. We made sure we got something useful ourselves. I was lucky to get a collared grey jersey knitted in thick oiled wool by our 'Canadian Friends'. It was not very sartorial but that was the least of our worries. Other treasures were the 'seaboot stockings' knitted in a similar white wool.

We sailed in the second half of November 1941. I remember the noise of the turbines starting up, thinking "I shall never get used to this!" but of course one does. It's like a mild form of titinitus—one only realises it's there when it stops. At that time the Arctic convoys had not been running long enough to gain a reputation and it's likely not many people had heard of them. The first of them, PQ1 had sailed on September 26th 1941 and others followed at about two weekly intervals. We were to be PQ5. I think there was one more before the end of the year, which went to Murmansk.

We joined a convoy going north up the East Coast, our destination Iceland. I think the Old Man and the Chief Engineer had been told that we must be prepared to discharge using only our own facilities and so they arranged to have a close inspection made of the deck winches. Soon afterwards it was discovered that a crosshead on one of them was cracked. Signals were made to the Commodore and not long after we were told to detach from the convoy off the Orkneys and go into Kirkwall.

In the meantime we got a bit of sea going experience. The Captain's name was Reevely, initial 'P' for Percy, and since he had a slight stammer he was known as P-P-P- Percy. Rather short in stature, he was a bit short fused and had that aggressiveness which seems common to small men. Dick had sailed with him before on the St. Helena and gave the opinion that it was important to stand up to him and refuse to be bullied—some advice to the junior apprentice! Poor young Bluey, who was the officer of my watch, was fairly terrified of him and was indeed harassed, but then, he was not all that competent. The Old Man had the bridge watch kept on the 'monkey island' above the wheelhouse—nothing wrong with that except that the only protection against the weather was a canvas screen about four feet high. He really should have got Chippy to do a proper job with a wind deflecting 'dodger'.

As far as we two 'lads' were concerned, the Old Man treated us very well. We had a few passengers, one of whom was a RAF Flt. Lt. Hurricane pilot, whose role we gathered was to familiarise the Ruskies with the planes we were carrying. He also kept bridge watch with us on the eight to twelve. I felt rather embarrassed at times when the Old Man stormed up the ladder and had a go at poor Bluey, yet was always courteous to the RAF type and myself.

When we anchored at Kirkwall the Old Man decided that Dick and I should take the winch part ashore to be repaired. Why he chose the two of us I don't know—just generosity to us two 'lads' I think. Arrangements were made with some workshop ashore. The next morning a boat was summoned and with a few shillings victualling allowance we set off. We soon found the workshop and we were told to come back there at three o'clock in the afternoon. The sun shone throughout a most pleasant day. I remember little else except that Kirkwall was so untouched by hostilities, although Scapa Naval Base was only just across the bay! Eggs, cream, butter and cheese seemed freely available and we fed well.

Upon reaching Iceland we called at Reykjavik where the Old Man went ashore to confer, and then we went further up the west coast to Hvalfford which was the convoy assembly port. Here we met up with our fellow travellers and on 27th November 1941 sailed northwards as Convoy PQ5. There were seven merchant ships, five British and two Russian, with an escort of three or four small RN minesweepers, I think a couple of destroyers and the cruiser Sheffield. We were amazed to see that the cook on one of the Russian ships was a woman and we gazed at her as intently as she gazed at us.

During the forenoon watch the Icelandic coastal scenery became very dramatic, with ice cliffs, snowfields and glaciers appearing in the very clear visibility. The night watch was accompanied by a vast and moving display of the Northern Lights such as I have never seen before nor since. It became colder. Dick and I took no part in the navigation on this voyage, as I had done on the St. Merriel and looking back I can't recall doing anything but bridge watch and signalling. I do know that on turning the corner of northwest Iceland and heading north and eastwards the Old Man and officers became increasingly concerned by the erratic behaviour of our magnetic compasses. The weather had become overcast and with no sight of the sun or horizon we could neither get a fix nor establish the compass error. No one knew how near we were to the northern ice and we just hoped that the RN escort with its radar and gyrocompasses was better informed. One morning we had warning to open out our convoy columns to pass either side of a huge block of ocean ice. It looked most sinister and it is said that there is seven times as much below the water than is visible above!

When the weather did clear somewhat, always there was a Blohm und Voss scout plane flying around the convoy just out of gun range. Jerry thus knew we were there, but fortunately for us at that stage of the war he was not in a position to do much about it, although we didn't actually know that. Occasionally, one or two of the escorts would give a reassuring depth charge display and once or twice did so with a large black flag hoisted, which we assumed meant that they had a firm contact. I understand that in the early days the Asdic operators had problems interpreting signals from the cold water layers of differing density. Otherwise all was quiet, but it got colder still.

I can't remember for sure what happened to the two Russian ships, but they perhaps turned south to Murmansk, whilst our small section of five ships carried on eastwards. We knew then that we were headed for Archangel and maybe the Old Man had known all along. The weather was fine with a few snow showers and in a couple of days we were at the entrance to the White Sea. Here was ice, nothing but ice and a couple of Russian ice breakers, one large, the other small. The escort left us. We stuck there in the ice for a while whilst the 'powers that be' worked out a plan of campaign. We lesser mortals looked at each other with misgivings.

When we saw the large breaker Lenin begin to move about breaking up the ice we knew that if we entered this inlet we would never get out unaided—the ice was already a couple of feet thick. The technique was for both breakers to move about and break up the ice around a ship. It was then that we realised how big and powerful the Lenin was; dimensionally she was almost as large as we were. They drove their bows up on to the ice and their weight broke through it with dramatic crunches and growls. She then passed to us a short towing spring, which was made fast to the windlass and mooring bits and she moved off dragging us through the ice. It had to be done fairly quickly, on a short towrope with little space between us, because the ice between the two ships welded together again as soon as it touched. The Old Man and the Mate went up and peered over the foc'sle head to see what effect this was having on our bow plating but the Ruskies were not concerned.

Since we moved in stages one ship at a time up the river Dvina, we lost track of the other ships but eventually three of us met up again, not at Archangel after all but at a small inlet on the opposite side called Bakaritza (my phonetic spelling). There, both ice breakers manoeuvred about making an icy mush and then dragged and pushed us alongside a timber pile jetty. We had arrived. No mooring ropes were strictly necessary although we did put some out— it didn't look right without them. Immediately there appeared a Russian sentry at the bottom of the gangway armed with a rifle and a very long bayonet. No one was allowed ashore but it didn't look very inviting anyway, nothing was there except more snow and ice, not a hut or a building in sight. Eventually we became one of three British ships frozen in there alongside that quay for the winter.

I think the other two British ships may have gone to Severodonisk (later called Molotovosk), which was a small military port west of where the river Dvina widens out.

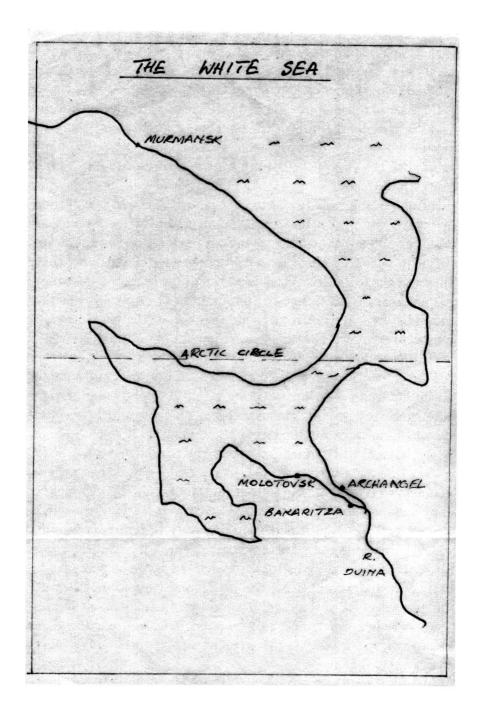

By now everything had frozen up. There was no running water to our washbasin or shower and no flushing lavatory; it was back to buckets again! To quote from Paul Kemp's book Convoy! Drama in Arctic Waters: "By the end of the year (1941) there were seven outward and four homeward convoys. Fifty-three ships were escorted to Russia and thirty-four returned. Archangel was selected because it was further away from the German bases in Norway. However, it was not ice-free. Soviet icebreakers worked hard to keep the Gourlo open until December the twelfth for the arrival of PQ5. The next convoy had to go to Murmansk. As a result five of the seven merchantmen in the convoy had to overwinter. We were one of them. By the end of the year the PQs had delivered 1400 lorries, 800 aircraft and 600 tanks, together with tons of stores and ammunition".

The intense cold showed up the deficiencies in our duffel coats. They were made with three layers: the outer one of a fine orange coloured canvas, the inner was reminiscent of a grey army blanket and in between was a layer of what today would be plastic film. Of course, in those days plastic as we know it did not exist, so what it really was I don't know. Whatever it was, it hadn't been 'researched and developed' for use in the arctic cold—it just went stiff and brittle and broke up into small pieces, which dropped down into the bottom hem of the coat. The outer layer, which was not waterproof, absorbed moisture and then froze stiff and hard.

We hoisted the derricks, stripped the hatches, and the Soviet mafia came aboard. They obviously wanted what we had brought as quickly as they could get it out, but in no way seemed inclined to be friendly. It was by now dark twenty four hours of the day, so we had to rig clusters of lights to allow work to get under way, and when the dockers did start they really went at it with little regard for our tackle. What we hadn't seen when we arrived, because of the snow covering, was that not too far off and running parallel with the quay was a railway siding. Beyond that again, invisible because it was sunk between snow banks on either side, were a roadway and a railway track. It was via these facilities that our cargo was taken away.

The St. Clears was mainly a riveted ship although some parts of the superstructure, including the Samson posts at number three hold, were welded. The fitting that carried the weight of the derrick and any cargo hanging therefrom was welded to the head of the post. Showing considerable prescience, the Mate instructed the Bosun to pass double wire strops through the fittings and around the outside of the posts as a safety measure. It was as well that he did. The cargo in the bottom of number three hold consisted of artillery shells of about 100 mm. calibre, which the Ruskies were hauling out in wire net slings with a married purchase and not too carefully. With a loud bang and a shudder, a piece of metal as big as a man's fist, to which the fitting was welded, ripped out of the steel post. The wire strops held.

Much later when I attended a course on welding, we were told how the intense heat used in the welding process can cause local stresses to be set up in the material, unless the heat is dissipated over a larger area. Perhaps that had not been done, the intense cold had intensified the stresses and some bucko Russian winch driving had done the rest. Full marks to the Mate—we might have had a catastrophe. By working two shifts, with Dick and I doing one each, the cargo was cleared just before Christmas. We cleared ship and covered the hatches as though we were to start a voyage, except that we couldn't wash down, only shovel off the snow and ice.

We were issued with shore passes, printed in the Cyrillic script. Every time we had to go ashore and for whatever reason, they were minutely examined by the sentry. Usually they were handed back without comment and I've wondered since whether most of the sentries could read but on one occasion, after looking hard at my pass, one of them said "Ah! Ivan! Kamarad!"

There was a British Army contingent present somewhere near Archangel whose function, so we were told, was to service the vehicles and equipment before they were handed over, but the Ruskies were so keen to get the stuff into use that they would not allow this and immediately took it away. I remember seeing a British squaddie, probably a despatch rider, trying not very successfully and with legs projecting out on either side, to ride his motor bike on the hard packed snow and ice roadway. It seemed so absurd.

The Bosun fell ill and the Mate put Dick in his place, a role that he enjoyed tremendously. At the same time thoughts were concentrated on how we could make ourselves more comfortable for the months to come. We had few resources, but we did have a good quantity of two inch by two-inch timber and some rolls of hessian. The Mate asked Chippy to erect, as well as he could, a timber framework around the accommodation and cover it with hessian to create an insulating air gap. He put me to help him.

Chips was quite young, about mid twenties, and had served his time as a shipwright. He carried his tools in a circular holdall, with the handle of his adze passing through the bag handles and swung over his shoulder in the approved manner. He had a broad Geordie accent and the good-humoured arrogance that some craftsmen have towards the unskilled. When I went and told him the Mate had sent me to help he gave the impression that he would put up with me, and I was very much the 'holder-upper'. Gradually we got to know each other, on a couple of occasions in an emergency I was allowed to use his saw and he found that I could use it as well as he could. When I told him that before going to sea I'd been learning to be a pattern maker we became pals and if ever he wanted a helper he would ask the Mate if he could have 'Harl'. He taught me how to use his adze. It was said that a good shipwright could trim his toe-nails with one and those who weren't so good trimmed their toes!

My first task each morning before breakfast was to go up on to the monkey island, read the outdoor temperature and enter it into the log. It was on New Year's morning that I learned the practical way that -40 degrees Centigrade is the same as -40 degrees Fahrenheit, for that is what the temperature was. That was the coldest I recorded. Everything froze—eye lashes, eye brows, nose drips, moustaches, beards. It was dangerous to touch metal with bare hands because one's skin instantly welded to it like instant glue. Our exhalations of breath froze around our nostrils, our eyebrows became covered with white frost and water from our eyes froze on our lids and cheeks. At least it was a change from Welsh coal dust. We discovered the layered look. This comprised long johns, two or three pairs of trousers, all the jerseys we had, whatever socks would fit into wellies or seaboots—and that was indoors! We relied upon activity to keep warm outside!

Our cabin, with its door and porthole opening directly on to the boat deck, would have been fine on voyages to South America but now it was not so hot. Fortunately our bunks were along the inside bulkhead or wall, which was formed by the engine room trunking, so with clean long johns and jerseys under our pyjamas it was possible to get warm and to sleep, otherwise the cabin was uninhabitable. A layer of frost about a centimetre thick gathered on the uninsulated interior of the outer bulkhead. With the light on it sparkled and looked quite pretty, but that was not an attraction we needed.

Back on the St. Merriel the captain, chief engineer, deck officers and sparks had taken their meals in the saloon dining room, but the other engineers (and the apprentices) had fed in the engineers' mess, so illustrating and perpetuating the traditional rivalry that was supposed to exist between the deck officers and the engineers. Certainly this did exist to some extent—there was a saying that oil and water don't mix. As a 'deck' apprentice I would have put this down to an inferiority complex on the part of some engineers, but of course they would have said it was a superiority complex on the part of the deck officers.

On the St. Clears and sister ships that carried passengers, the demarcation line was drawn differently. The Old Man and Chief ate in the saloon with the passengers; deck officers, engineers, sparks and the apprentices dined in the officers' mess. I thought this a much better arrangement, spoiled only by the meanness of the mess, which was too small. It had a table with places for eight and nothing more. During our stay in Russia the three mates, three engineers and chief sparks went in to first sitting, leaving the second sitting to the two junior sparks and us two 'boys', although Bluey often joined us as well as he preferred our company. When the evening meal was over the Mate and Second Mate disappeared and usually were not seen again—Dick and I thought they were of the opinion that to consort with engineers and juniors was socially beneath them. The smallness of the mess was now an asset, particularly as its door was opposite the door to the engine room and with both doors open we got some of its heat. Our 'second sitting' took to spending the evenings there, to be joined by all the engineers and the Chief Sparks.

By this stage of the war merchant ships carried three radio operators, the two juniors usually being youngsters who had taken a course and were in 'for the duration'. Now, our three had practically nothing to do except to check the batteries and equipment every so often. The Second Sparks named Cyril was unusually old for this position, about thirty, and came from a north country family, which in those pre-television days had, like many others, made its own entertainment consisting of music, board games, card games and so on. He decided that with a long stay in prospect we needed to get organised. Under his guidance and supervision we made draughts, chess, Ludo and most successfully, Monopoly. Those of us who could draw and model made the board, houses and hotels, printed the money, penalties and rewards. It became very popular and everybody could join in at the start of a game, those who went bankrupt attaching themselves to someone else as 'treasurer'. It became very competitive and vociferous and towards the end when there were only two or three left in they would have 'banks' to conduct and watch over their business. Games would start as soon as the steward had cleared off the table and sometimes they would still be going on at midnight.

Chippy provided me with some plywood and with the loan of his tenon saw I made a set of Mah-jong tiles, which Cyril's memory for that sort of thing enabled us to complete, but it was never as popular as Monopoly.

We played a lot of Bridge. The Chief Engineer joined our messroom group and he was a good player, as was his Fourth who was older than most of that rank. He had been working ashore, but his job ended after the war started and he had been directed back to sea. He was one of those unfortunate people who was sick every time the ship left harbour. Between the two of them they taught us youngsters the game from first principles.

Just before Christmas it was discovered that there was a small camp of Polish army officers in the vicinity. Captured by the Russians during the invasion of eastern Poland, the officers had become prisoners of war. As the Poles were already our allies, and we were now allies of the Russians, the Poles were de facto no longer the enemies of Russia and had been set free inasmuch as they were no longer confined to the prison camp. The gates were open but where could they go? It seemed to us that the Russian hierarchy was not even concerned about the well being of it's own people and was certainly not going to worry about the fate of a few Poles. They were in dire straits, with not much food and unable to do anything about it.

Someone, and the initiative may have come from the masters of our three British ships, thought we should help by inviting them to share our Christmas dinner. This we did, with much clicking of heels and many toasts in vodka to our families, motherlands and victory. They were in a sad predicament, their eastern lands overrun by the Russians and their western territories by the Germans. They were desperately worried about the fate of their families.

A little later in the New Year the Poles invited us to their camp for a concert. They had collected, as we ourselves did later, some musical instruments and made up a small band. As we were walking there in the evening, a light-hearted incident happened. It was very dark of course and one of the sparkies, who was larking about, strayed off the hard-packed snow road and sank up to his armpits in the soft snow. We managed to extricate him.

At the camp there was much singing of national and patriotic songs—the Poles were much better at that sort of thing than we were. National anthems and of course many more toasts were well fuelled by vodka. They were moved later on and we often wondered what fate befell them.

10

F*** JOE STALIN!

Life in the workers' democracy

From the ship's side amidships, warm water was discharged from the engine room condenser into the frozen river. Now that we were offloaded, the outlet was probably about eight feet above the water line and because the discharge was warm it kept a semicircle of ice-free water, about fifteen feet across, against the ships side. This was very convenient as into it went all our rubbish, there being nowhere else for it to go—kitchen waste, engine room waste, human waste, the lot.

When the cargo was out the Ruskies cleared off and left us, but early in the New Year gangs of slave workers arrived with their overseers to rebuild the log surface of the quay. The quay was built in a kind of log cabin form—criss-cross logs fitted together with a type of cross halving joint cut out with an axe. The top two or three layers were removed and replaced by new ones.

Our seamen established that the workers were political prisoners although I cannot vouch for that, certainly they were prisoners of some sort. They were under the control of armed guards and any misdemeanour got a thump between the shoulder blades with a rifle butt. They were not allowed to talk to our men but of course the guards could not stop our men talking to the prisoners. They couldn't speak English, neither could our men speak Russian, but language difference is no problem to an English sailor. They were obviously very hungry, if not starving, and our men would surreptitiously pass to them what was left from their meals and anything else they had.

To move the logs about, a rope was fastened to one end. A small gang of workers would put the other end over their shoulders and heave it along a yard or two at a pull, chanting something that sounded like, "Rous, dva, dali", in the same way that we would say, "One, two, heave". For encouragement our men would line our ships rail and in unison with them shout, "Fuck, Joe, Stalin", to be greeted by grins and calls of "Kamarad!"

If one or two could slip their guards they would drop down on to the ice, sneak around to our offside and fish with sticks in the condenser discharge water for anything they thought might be edible. The steward had obtained from somewhere a few head of poultry (we may have carried them with us) and these were cleaned and cooked for our New Year dinner, the guts and waste being dumped into the aforesaid pool. It had by then acquired a thin covering film of black oil. No matter, I saw two prisoners fish these scraps out and eat them raw on the spot, only to be caught by the guards and thumped unmercifully for their success.

The ice on the River Dvina was now four or five feet thick. From our bridge it was possible to see in the distance, on the opposite side of the river, the city of Archangel and most of the width of the river in front of it, with people, horses and carts and lorries constantly crossing in both directions over the ice. The more adventurous of the crew began to explore. No one drew any money: for one thing there was very little to spend it on and secondly there was a thriving black market, which quite naturally the crew exploited. I believe soap was the major item of currency but I've no doubt that a fair amount of the ship's other commodities went the same way. One fireman had so much cash he was known as the Mayor of Bakaritza and was reputed to be a rouble millionaire.

Someone found a shop in Archangel that sold musical instruments. It was so strange to find something worthwhile for sale that the crew bought some, including a trumpet, a violin and a number of stringed twangy instruments. I suggested to my friend Chippy that I would like to attempt to learn to play a Russian mandolin and in a few days one appeared—no problem, no charge. (It's now at home up in the loft). I was able to play popular tunes, since the tuning is the same as for a violin, but not having a very good 'ear' I had to learn them by rote.

Every so often the Mate and the Second Engineer would equip all the seamen and firemen with steel bars, sledge hammers and such like and attempt to break the ice around the ship, so that we did not get 'pinched'. The area around the stern was given serious attention, the screw being partly out of the ice as was much of the rudder. The worry was that moving ice pressure might damage them. When with difficulty the ice had been cleared, the Engineer would give the screw a few revolutions ahead and astern. One result of this was a wash of fresh water over the surrounding area, which instantly froze into a beautifully smooth skating rink. Skates were available from the usual black market sources and crude ice hockey matches took place. Bluey, the Nova Scotian immediately became the star. Virtually brought up on skis, snowshoes and skates, he was in his element.

We, that is a few of us youngsters, made two or three excursions to Archangel, mainly for the hell of it. The journey there and back was a challenge in itself. One could walk there and back, which I guess was a round trip of perhaps six miles, or one could go to a bend in the sunken rutted road and wait on the snow bank for an empty slow moving lorry and jump in the back. The drivers didn't mind and one might be lucky enough to jump on one that was crossing the river. One could also go to the railway. The small steam engines used short wood logs for fuel and these were stored in dumps by the track. If one waited at the dump quite near to the ship, sooner or later a wagon train would come along that needed to refuel and a lift was obtainable. The snag with both these last two methods was that it was terribly cold waiting—it was more comfortable to walk.

We found little or nothing in Archangel to interest us, or if there was we didn't know of it. We would call into the Intourist Hotel for a glass or two of Russian tea. That was all right but the place stank so much from bad sewage and lack of ventilation that we were always glad to get out again. On one evening we went to the theatre where a travelling company was putting on one of Chekhov's plays. We knew it would be in Russian, of which we understood not a word, but thought that maybe we could pick up something from the action. Not a thing!

Dick and I both had 'steady' girl friends and so were not active in seeking out the opposite sex. It didn't look very enticing. Both sexes looked the same anyway. All wore felt boots with quilted baggy trousers tucked into them, bum length jackets of the same construction, or some wore a full-length coat. One could tell the male from the female in two ways. Firstly, men were usually bigger than women. Secondly, the men wore a fur or astrakhan hat with pull down earflaps, whilst the women wore scarves over their heads which were tied under the chin. This hid all of the face except the nose and eyes. The general shape was square and dumpy with a round blob on the top.

Between the ship (but out of sight of it) and the river crossing point was a small settlement. It consisted of a few timber buildings, plus two much larger three storied log-built ones, looking rather like barracks. The young and adventurous in our crew said that these were hostels for young women workers, who were willing, and told stirring tales of five in a bed and such like. Dick and I looked at each other and thought that from what we've seen they're welcome. Not until the spring and early summer came and the girls turned out in bright cotton frocks, did we realise that under that welter of insulation there might well be a lissom Russian wench.

One afternoon, still in the winter, as we walked through this settlement we saw that the gable end of one of the 'barracks' had burst open, cascading out into the street a vast heap of human ordure, by then shiny and frozen hard. Presumably, when it was no longer frozen inside, the pressure had built up to more than the structure could withstand. A bizarre sight!

At the beginning of the voyage we had been stored and fuelled for three months and now we were getting short of both. From the galley wireless, we gathered that the Old Man was having difficulty in persuading the Russians to supply us with anything and that the other two British ships with us were in the same predicament. I have to say this. At that time the Russians were the most ungrateful, least co-operative, stubborn and suspicious people we had ever met and if we could have loaded our cargo back on board and brought it home we would have done.

Eventually we got some food comprising rice, fish about the size and shape of cricket bats and just as hard, but which turned out to be quite good when thawed and cooked, and frozen carcasses of some small four legged animals which we thought may have been small deer. We didn't much mind what they were. The small British Army contingent, which was intended to service the vehicles we of-floaded, was able to give some stores to us. From now on our food became rather boring but we didn't starve.

Fuel was a different matter since no water borne tanker could get to us. The Russians said they could get some rail tankers on to the quay if we could get the oil aboard. A scheme was devised to mount two forty gallon oil drums with one end cut out on to a trolley, so that oil from the rail tanker could be run in to them and then they could be trundled slightly down hill to the ship. Chippy and I made a rugged landing table about three feet high that was positioned on deck close to the ship's side. Below this was mounted another cut down drum with a pipe fitting attached to the bottom, about four inches in diameter, to be used as a funnel and from which the en-gineers led a flexible hose to the ship's fuel inlet. The idea was that the drums would be hoisted on board by one of our derricks and the oil poured into the 'funnel'. The engineers even contrived a steam heating coil in it to reduce the viscosity of the oil so that it would run freely. Alas (or maybe thank goodness) it was all unnecessary—when the oil was delivered it was so 'light' and the viscosity so low that it was possible to pump it aboard by hand.

I don't know whose idea it was but with the blessing of the Chief, Dick and I were sent to work in the engine room for a couple of weeks to 'increase our engineering experience'. I don't remember whether we did much work but it made a nice change to be somewhere warm.

Sometime in January a bit of daylight began to creep back for a slowly lengthening period and by the end of February it was light from about eight in the morning until four in the afternoon. Mail got through to us, but not often and when it did all was silent for a while. From our ship's newsheet we learned that the war was hotting up, particularly on the North Atlantic and Arctic convoy routes. We felt rather left out of things, as indeed we were.

The Mate sent Dick and I into the 'tween decks to check over and repair any defects in the derrick gear. Here we found a new pastime. Although the ship had been fumigated in the UK we discovered that there were a few rats in the holds sheltering under the dunnage boards—they had probably come aboard with the ballast. We would open up the hatch to let in some light, arm ourselves with cudgels and turn over the boards. When a rat was disturbed we would chase it to extinction or until it escaped, whooping like Red Indians. It was quite mad really but it was one way of letting off steam.

A serious shortage for some people was that of tobacco, cigarettes and cigarette paper. Most sailors who smoked 'rolled their own' using Capstan Fine Cut flake tobacco, which at five shillings for half a pound was cheap and a very good smoke. When that gave out I gave up, but others found it more difficult or even impossible. Russian cigarettes were not very much liked and seemed to consist of about one and a half inches of cigarette plus the same length of cardboard tube. Most people preferred to re-cycle their 'dogends' but they got a bit strong after re-rolling. It was then that people discovered that there was more to cigarette paper than just its thinness. If ordinary thin paper was used a swift inhalation could cause the end of the cigarette to burst into flame. One of the firemen was reputed to have the best cigarette paper in Bakaritza. This was a pocket size prayer book and before 'rolling one' he was likely to read a collect or a psalm, or anything else uplifting prior to tearing out the page.

In April the Old Man sent for Dick and I and we wondered why.

It was to say that he had our third year exam papers and we were to sit them next week in the saloon. The Chief Steward would look after us. Our cabin was habitable again by then and we attempted a bit of revision. It was then that I became aware of Dick's problem with trigonometry and algebra. If the question was straightforward he was all right but if it required transposing the formula he was sunk. I tried to help, but he had the habit of throwing up his arms and saying, "It's no use, I can't do it", and that was that. One of the papers called 'Knowledge of Principles' consisted mostly of that kind of thing and when we came to the exam Dick just read it and walked out.

By the end of April the weather was changing. There was more daylight, with a bit of warmth in the sun causing puddles of water to form on the ice. Some time in May 1942 we became aware that the traffic crossing the river had stopped and later the pedestrians ceased too. Towards the end of the month the ice in the main river began to crack and break up. Slowly it began to move, although nothing happened at first in our inlet, and then gradually the process speeded up. Soon huge blocks of ice were moving past at considerable speed—I remember seeing one large enough to be carrying a fair size wooden building and I wondered if it was empty. Whole trees went careering seawards together with all sorts of debris.

When the main river Dvina was clear, which took several weeks, we raised steam and a pilot came aboard. One of the small icebreaker tugs cleared the water around us and we made our way out of the creek across the river to one of the waterside berths at Archangel, there to load sawn timber, softwood, machined boarding and paper pulp. It was now, when the sun shone, that we became aware of the lasses in their cotton frocks. The mosquitoes, the biggest and most ferocious I ever came across, emerged and we were stung all over.

The loading of timber took place during the daytime, but for some reason unknown to us the paper pulp went into number four hold at night-time. Being the junior apprentice I was put on nights, which was not onerous with only one hatch being worked. Paper pulp is like soft cardboard and is either made up into compressed rolls or rectangular bales: in this case it was bales measuring about four feet by three feet by one foot and they were quite heavy. They were loaded in by shore crane, four at a time in a rope sling and the stowage which I had to supervise was done by a small gang of schoolgirls of about thirteen or fourteen years of age.

The girls had to roll the bales over and over and manoeuvre them tightly into place. Their leader was a nice young lass who spoke a few words of English but not enough for a conversation, although I've realised since that with such mutual distrust they may have been prohibited from conversing with us. The steward used to leave me quite a large plate of sandwiches to keep body and soul together during the small hours. At about 2 a.m. when the girls had their break, I felt so sorry for them that I used to take the sandwiches down into the hold and share them around. What they thought of white bread sandwiches cut in 'English diagonal style' with no crusts I don't know, but there was never any refusal. This work was not what young girls should have been doing at that hour, but I suppose it was for Uncle Joe and the motherland.

Someone arranged for us to play a British Army team at soccer. Dick (as senior apprentice, ha! ha!) was told or volunteered to get our team organised. The match took place one afternoon on a rather rough pitch. I remember two things only. The first was what I thought to be the unnecessary aggressiveness of the army team. I had been taught that playing the game with skill was the essential thing—if one won so much the better, but there was no need to go berserk about it, it was not the end of the world to lose. The second was rather painful. In the second half my opposing squaddie and I both ran for a loose ball. He got there about a yard before me and gave the ball a 'blinder' which hit me right in the crotch. On landing back on earth I collapsed in a crumpled heap of agony and was carried off to the sideline to recover. I did slowly and was able to return to the pitch to complete the match, but not very enthusiastically. I suppose we lost. For some days afterwards whenever I had to pee it was like passing broken bottles. I feared for my wrecked manhood but normality slowly returned.

I was on deck one afternoon when I became aware of a considerable stir along the waterfront and up the river came three or four US Liberty ships with large ensigns flying. They were the first ships to arrive that year (1942); they knew it and were absolutely delighted. They were part of convoy PQ16, which had been heavily attacked losing five ships, but they had fought their way through and made it to their destination. Since they were the first ships that year to go up the Dvina, the American's couldn't understand how we Limeys were already there. When they discovered that we had over wintered and were just about on our beam ends for smokes and stores they couldn't do enough for us. They showered us with cartons of cigarettes, cornflakes, dried milk, coffee and anything else they had. They couldn't speak too highly of the RN escort, particularly the anti aircraft cruiser, which was one of the converted 'Bank' boats that I mentioned earlier. One of them said to me "Boy! Did that ship throw some shit!" This certainly looked impressive, but we knew that the deciding factor was always the determination of the attacking pilots.

From somewhere came the news that owing to the shortage of deck officers, the required sea-time experience of four years before sitting the Second Mate's Examination was being reduced to three years and six months. This meant that Dick already had his time completed. The question was, would I complete mine by the time we got back? It looked very much like it but it would be a close run thing. If so, would the Company release us from our Indentures?

Came the time to leave and not a tear was shed. By then it was the second half of June. When we had arrived there in mid December it was all darkness and ice, now it was all daylight and the White Sea was engulfed in fog. We must have relied upon the Royal Navy again for the navigation. After a few days on passage, the Murmansk contingent came out and we joined up to form into QP13, for some an unlucky number. Thirty-five ships left in the convoy for home, sailing on June 28th 1942.

Still the fog continued, not so thick that it was dangerous in the convoy but usually enough to keep us from the prying eyes of the Luftwaffe, although the Blohm und Voss did find us occasionally. By this time some intelligent soul had invented, and we were all provided with, a remarkably good fog buoy. When towed astern at the required two cables length it provided a very good marker for the ship next astern by throwing up a small fountain of water. I have attempted a drawing to show how it worked—like most good ideas it was very simple. Until that time ships had towed all sorts of objects with little success, the first recommendation being a small wooden barrel. It was really surprising to us how most things, when towed, wanted to hide away just beneath the surface.

On July 2nd, unseen and unknown to us to the north east of Jan Mayen Island, we passed the outward-bound convoy PQ17. Blohm und Voss found us both and then concentrated on the potentially more rewarding outward bound convoy, which following a disastrous mistake by the Admiralty was hounded to destruction. Paul Kemp writes that this disaster obscured the fate of what happened to our westbound QP13 of thirty-five ships. "On July 4th the convoy divided off Iceland, sixteen ships turning south for Loch Ewe (that was us), the remaining nineteen round the north of Iceland for Reykjavik. In bad weather they lost position and ran on to a minefield. Five ships were sunk and one damaged". Yet again I had been lucky.

Loch Ewe was a wonderful sight: I remember the gannets, or maybe they were cormorants or shags, diving on to a shoal of mackerel. From there we convoyed uneventfully to Hull. I had my time in by now and Dick and I asked for release from our indentures, which was allowed. Since we had become good pals, we decided that we would go together to the Nautical Department of the Technical College at Cardiff and sit the Second Mates' Exam there. It was reasonable travelling distance from both our hometowns and the College had a good reputation.

There was a short period of tension. Somehow Dick had got his number one uniform into a bit of a mess. I still remember going up to our cabin on Christmas night to find Dick already turned in, dressed complete in uniform and still with his cap on! He didn't want to go home and meet his girl friend dressed in civvies—she was a nurse and would want to show him off, especially as the northern convoys had been in the news—so he decided to wash it. He should have had more sense! He put it in a bucket of hot water with some soda and when he lifted it out later most of the colour was left behind in the bucket. It had become a kind of reddish brown camouflage. Fortunately a Jewish sweatshop tailor came aboard that afternoon and promised to make him a 'made to measure' in two days. He did, and Dick went home to a hero's welcome.

I went home on leave too to find that I had done quite well in the third year exams, which was a confidence booster, though I was disappointed with my effort in Navigation where I thought I was quite strong. I can't remember any events from my leave except to say that my love for and admiration of Edna became stronger and stronger as time passed.

Thinking back to this Russian episode it had two things in its favour, which at the time we did not appreciate. Firstly, there were times when we may not have been very comfortable up there but we were out of harms way. Early 1942 was a time when the Germans mounted one of their heaviest offensives against allied shipping. In the first seven months 4.7 million tons worldwide went down, 3.3 million tons sunk by submarine and 3.3 million tons of it in the North Atlantic. June proved to be the worst month of the war.

The second advantage I have already mentioned. During the whole of the voyage of eight months and nineteen days, neither Dick nor I drew any money so we each had a large pay-off of about a hundred pounds. This was quite a sum then! It secured my immediate future.

Since writing this chapter I came across a book called 'The Voyages of Discovery' by Ann Savours (Chatham Pub.), which stated that in 1915 Scott's old ship the Discovery sailed as a freighter, carrying goods from Brest to Archangel, arriving there on October 15th. " Steamer No.141—Discovery—discharged her 500 tons of cargo at the Russian government berth of Bakaritsya. She was fortunate to depart for Le Havre before the freezing of the Dvina and the White Sea". Obviously she was luckier than us, but just think, we may have lain in the berth of the old Discovery and didn't know it!

23. *When all else was done there was always rust to be chipped off the deck, but not between 1 & 3pm. when watch keepers below had a shuteye.*

24. *On leave with Edna 1940.*

25. *On Monkey Island using the dry card compass and azimuth mirror –*
a horizontal prism – to take bearings. The circular structure behind is the
useless direction finder aerial.

26. *Atop the foremast and ser-*
vicing the ballon fitting.

27. Semaphore practice.

28. One of the Hotchkiss machine guns.

29. *Second Mate Hy. Gittins taking his morning sights.*

30. *The young apprentice does likewise.*

31. A convoy assembles at Milford Haven. Some ships have balloons flying. Courtesy of Imperial War Museum. A 8187

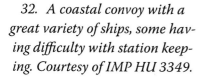

32. A coastal convoy with a
great variety of ships, some having difficulty with station keeping. Courtesy of IMP HU 3349.

33. *Buenos Aires, Sunday morning, I saw this schooner approaching and thinking it would make a good photograph ran to get the 'Box Brownie'. When I returned just in time Chief Officer Ellis was there to make a very good picture.*

34. *Arthur and I ready to go ashore in Rio.*

35. *The Saint Merriel in Salford docks, topmasts lowered to pass beneath bridges, completed discharging, high out of the water and looking very weather beaten and drab in overall grey.*

36. *Daylight morse signalling.*

37. *This postcard is of the St. Clears on her trials. Directly below the funnel, half way up the hull is a horizontal white mark – the load line, below that and to left is the condenser discharge.*

38. *An arctic convoy assembling at Hvalford, Iceland.*
IWM A 9172.

39. A liberty ship in heavy weather. IWM A 27565.

40. Convoy steaming through pack ice. IWM N 15360.

41. *The ice getting thicker. A US(?) merchantman simply bristling with light ack ack. IWM 15358*

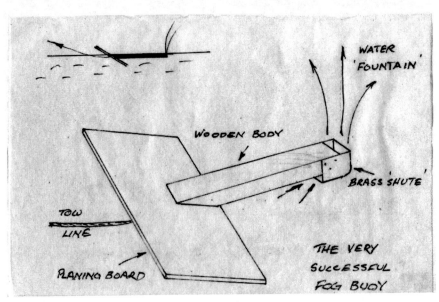

WATER
'FOUNTAIN'

WOODEN BODY

BRASS 'SHUTE'

TOW
LINE

PLANING BOARD

THE VERY
SUCCESSFUL
FOG BUOY

42. *Drawing of Fog Buoy.*

„СОРОК ЛЕТ ПОБЕДЫ
В ВЕЛИКОЙ ОТЕЧЕСТВЕННОЙ ВОЙНЕ
1941—1945 гг."

УДОСТОВЕРЕНИЕ

Холл И.

ВРУЧЕНА ЮБИЛЕЙНАЯ МЕДАЛЬ

„СОРОК ЛЕТ ПОБЕДЫ
В ВЕЛИКОЙ ОТЕЧЕСТВЕННОЙ
ВОЙНЕ 1941—1945 гг."

Президент
Союз Советских
Социалистических Республик

31 - *ИЮЛЯ* 19 *91* года

0859

УЧАСТНИКУ ВОЙНЫ

43. *The citation for the medal awarded during the Presidency of M. Gorbachov.*

44. *The lapel Arctic Badge quite recently awarded by HMG. Only 20mm. across in white, red and gold, in reality it looks more attractive than it does here.*

45. The beautiful Sunderland flying boat escorting a troop   convoy – and were we glad to see them with the reassurance that we were getting nearer to home! IWM CH 832.

46. The not so beautiful Catalina – but we were equally glad to   see them. IWM CH 2455

11

CARDIFFIAN INTERLUDE

Second Mate's Ticket

At the end of our leave some time in August 1942 Dick and I met up in Cardiff. We enrolled at the College and found digs. Exactly how we did this I can't remember for sure but after three years of war the country was much more regimented, organised and committed. Anyone with spare accommodation had to register it officially.

We were probably sent by the 'billeting officer'- and we were very lucky to be sent—to number 18, Conway Road, Canton. I can still remember the address now. It was a large semi-detached villa where lived Mrs. David, a widow. She lived with her daughter Mabel, who was single and whom one could call the housekeeper because although deferential to her mother it was Mabel who ran the household. Also there was Victor the son, a dandy, shy sort of a fellow, also single who worked in a bank (perhaps a reserved occupation?) and was in the Home Guard, but not enthusiastically.

They were a grand family who made us very welcome and put us into the large front bedroom where we could have a study table each. We ate with the family and for wartime we fed really well. There was also another lodger, an older man who worked in a bank, but he ate his meals on his own and was not seen much by us. Mrs.

David was a merry soul and clearly enjoyed having us youngsters to stay. We were, after all, well-behaved and certainly little trouble.

The Cathedral Road (Llandaff) tram terminus was just at the end of our road and a one penny tram ride of just over a mile took us to alight outside the castle, from where it was a short walk to the College in the Civic Centre. In those days, before the take-over of the city by the internal combustion engine, Cardiff was a very pleasant place to be and the Civic Centre with its modern classical style architecture was clean and spacious.

We had to pay for our accommodation, which was probably at a 'controlled' price. The College's tuition fees at this time were probably gratis, although I think we did have to pay the exam fee. We were allowed twelve weeks study time, during which the exams had to be taken. Although one could take as little time as desired, Dick and I agreed we were going to take the whole twelve weeks, since one didn't know when the next leave was going to turn up. Owing to the shortage of certified officers and to encourage more men to qualify, we could also draw unemployment benefit for a limited number of weeks. Nobody was throwing money at us, we had to dip into our savings, but the financial problems I had foreseen at the beginning of my time as an apprentice had not arisen.

The pattern of study at the college was a repeating twelve-week course cycle. Probably half a dozen people joined or left to sit the exams at two weekly intervals. They were a mixed bunch. Some were youngsters like us, just having completed their reduced qualifying time at sea. Some were a bit older, coming back for a re-sit, having failed the first time. Others were older still, perhaps ABs having a try to get out of the foc'stle and sometimes having a struggle. The atmosphere was quite intense and serious, with no time for social occasions as too much was at stake.

About two weeks into the course, the senior lecturer came over, sat beside me and asked when I was thinking of taking the exam. When I told him the date Dick and I had agreed on he was a bit concerned. He said that looking at my work, he thought I was well prepared already and I must be careful not to get stale. I assured him that I would not.

We would return to our digs in late afternoon, have our meal with the family, listen to the six o'clock news and then head up to the bedroom for a couple of hour's work. At about nine o'clock we would take a break and walk to the little pub on the corner for a swift half. We used the bar patronised by about half a dozen elderly regulars. There was a kind of Bagatelle table I have not seen elsewhere: it was about two feet wide, five feet long and had a semicircular end, covered and cushioned like a billiard table. There were hollows for the ball to drop into which scored points, a pocket on each side and two or three wooden obstacles like small mushrooms, which did not have to be knocked over. When the locals found out who we were and what we were doing they became quite friendly and were keen to teach us to play.

The main exam subjects were Navigation (two papers), Seamanship (two papers, one of them written and one viva voce), Knowledge of Principles (KoP), Ship Construction, Engineering Knowledge, plus one more which I forget. Of these, the most feared was the oral Seamanship exam—some examiners had a reputation for ferocity. There was an exam in Signalling (Light Morse, Semaphore and International Code of Signalling (flags)), which was not a problem to those of us who had had plenty of experience of wartime convoy signalling. The practical instruction classes were taken by a small rotund RN Chief Yeoman of Signals, whose line of patter was an entertainment worth sitting through. One had to obtain a lifeboat certificate, which again held no difficulty for us—we could have run this course ourselves.

We were also required to pass the St. John's Ambulance exam. This was so much a farce at Cardiff that it was a scandal. At each session the group under 'tuition' sat around what, years ago, was probably the surgery waiting room. The old doc' sat in a chair and mumbled incoherently for about half an hour, sucked his teeth, signed our cards and off we went. On the sixth occasion we were certified but not a bit wiser! Nobody thought that the St. John's had much to do with life at sea. It was reputed that the only candidate to fail had been asked what to do if a man was bleeding heavily from the head, and he had replied, "Put a tourniquet round his neck".

Weekends became a bit of a drag—we couldn't work all the time—but occasionally there would be a rugby match at Cardiff Arms Park, a play at the theatre and at one time a visit by one of the opera companies. Dick was an absolute philistine, but I persuaded him to see Die Fliedermaus and he was entranced. Even so, I couldn't get him along to any other cultural activity. We had a weekend or two off at home and Edna is convinced that she came down to Cardiff one weekend but that I failed to meet her on time at Cardiff station!

We met another ex Saint Line apprentice on the course, Robert Davies, an excellent chap who both saddened and worried me. He had been on the St. Elwyn when she was torpedoed in the Atlantic and as a result of exposure in the lifeboat, the tips of all his fingers and some of his toes had been lost through frostbite. After a period in hospital and a long convalescence, the Saint Line employed him in the office. What worried me was that he wanted to go back to sea again and although he was a bit short of sea-time, the company had obtained for him a dispensation to sit the exam. He had recovered well but I was saddened to see what the exposure had done to his physique.

Dick made poor progress, if any, with 'Knowledge of Principles'. I forget the details now of the exam marking, but some of the papers were 'failing papers'—fail the paper and one failed the whole exam. Some other papers one could re-sit, and if one failed the oral Seamanship the examiner could say how much more sea-time had to be served before re-sitting, maybe three months, six months or a year. This is probably another reason why it was feared so much.

I remember two incidents from the exam week. During my oral test the examiner produced a beautiful scale model of a ship's telescopic foremast and asked me to go through the procedure for lowering the topmast. Well, we had done this on the St. Merriel on each occasion that we had gone up the canal to Manchester and I knew the procedure thoroughly. It was, as they say, a gift!

Then, on the afternoon of the KoP exam we had been going for about twenty minutes, when I saw Dick get up, walk to the front and hand in his papers. He left the examination room and did not return. When I returned to the digs after the exam, Mabel said he had told her his mind had gone blank. He had packed all his belongings and left for home. I never saw or heard of him again. It was strange!

The following week the college told me I had passed all subjects. I sent off telegrams to my parents at Sandwell Avenue and to Edna. Robbie had failed the oral Seamanship paper and was given 'sea-time'. I have to say I was not sorry and hoped that the doctor would not pass him fit enough to return. The Saint Line had not done very well: of their three apprentices on the course, I was the only one to pass and I was not going to go back to them! I had done so much studying during the term of my apprenticeship I think I could have passed the exams without going to the College, but remember I started off with the intention to go there. That is not to say that I did not learn anything useful whilst I was there—I gained much in experience and a few months ashore was a relaxing respite before what was to come.

Edna came down to Cardiff to celebrate, not just my exam result but because we had agreed to get engaged. The Davids provided her with a room. From a shop in the arcade opposite the castle we bought the ring, for which I still have the receipt. Another purchase, this time from an instrument shop in dockland, was my first sextant—yes, we had to provide our own navigation tools—and from a tailor's I bought the first single gold stripe and epaulettes of 'rank'. I felt marvellous. I was twenty years old and I had taken the first step up. I'd even got the girl!

We had a very happy few days before I reported to the 'Pool' and we then went back home to await the future. I spent a total time of five months ashore.

12

THE POOL, REPLACEMENT SHIPS, BANGS & DEMS

Now we're getting organised

I had three options: I could tell the Saint Line that I had obtained my Second Mate's Certificate and ask them if they had a job for me, I could apply to some other company in the same way, or I could go on the 'Pool'. I'll try to explain.

All seamen had now become registered labour, as were all shore workers. Whereas the latter had to register at a local Employment Exchange, seamen registered at a Pool Office. There was one of these at all major ports and when signing off a ship seamen had to nominate the Pool at which they wished to register, which was usually their local port, but it did not have to be. There was no local port for Darlaston!

Leave was now regulated too, with no more laissez-faire. For officers, it was two and a half days a month, although it was probably the same for everyone else. It was paid too, but only at the basic rate, as war bonus was only paid when 'signed on'. The Master of a ship that needed a crew informed the local Pool, which looked at its register to see who was available and 'roped them in'. One did not necessarily have to accept the first ship offered by the Pool—I think one could refuse two, but had to accept the third. 'Company men' who were kept continuously employed did not have to keep reporting to the Pool, although they were also registered.

When my indentures closed I ceased to be employed by the Saint Line. I discovered during my time at the Cardiff College that there were ex-apprentices and cadets who were receiving a retainer from their previous company, to ensure that when they had completed the course (pass or fail) they returned. They did not have to draw unemployment pay. I had received nothing from the Saint Line. They had not wished me well, neither thanking me for three and a half years of conscientious work for little pay, nor suggesting that they would like me to continue working for them, let alone paying me a retainer. Since they had not paid me a retainer, I did not consider myself retained. I thought that if they were so indifferent to me, then I would be so to them, and when one is young one has strong ideas.

It so happened that about two months into my next voyage, I heard from Father saying that he had received a letter from the Saint Line asking what had happened to me. They said they had received such good reports of me that they hoped I would continue with them. I replied to Father that they should have thought of that earlier, which he didn't much like. Father was still living in the era when men thought themselves lucky if they had a job and did everything they could to keep it. No doubt he thought of some politic reply. Before the war started the shipping companies dictated the terms of employment, the Depression hit shipping very hard and seamen accepted harsh conditions in order to get a job. Times had changed and in my opinion the Saint Line hadn't realised that—seamen were now in short supply and they could 'pick and choose'.

In any case, I had resolved long before that what I ought to do at this stage of my career, for I was still intent on the sea, was to get as wide an experience as possible, by sailing with other companies on a variety of ships. For that reason I decided to take a chance on the Pool and see what turned up. It didn't turn out as I had intended, but no matter.

I'll digress here to say something about 'replacement ships'. Left to our own devices we would have lost the war, if only because of lack of shipping. More shipping was being lost than could be replaced, to say nothing of the crews. Enemy merchant ships, which were captured and used by us, were given a name preceded by 'Empire' and new ships, which were built here to a standard design, were similarly named.

Canada and the USA also built ships for us to a similar standard design and these ships' names had the prefix 'Fort' and 'Ocean' respectively. The USA also built their own replacement ships called 'Liberty' ships and those that were leased, chartered or loaned to Britain had the appropriate prefix of 'Sam'. It was these replacement ships which saved the free world—it's as simple as that!

There is a tendency now to denigrate these ships as being quick, cheap and nasty—they were nothing of the kind. Thank goodness they were quickly built and since revolutionary construction methods were used there was bound to be a problem or two, but on the whole they were good well-found ships. I have nothing but praise for them. We received 354 of the 'Fort' boats from Canada, many built on the West Coast. I was to join two of them just after they had come over to Europe, but I was not lucky enough to be sent to Vancouver fetch one, which would have involved crossing the Rockies by train. All the Fort and Ocean ships were, as far as I know, coal burners.

Since these ships were built during wartime, they were built for war service complete with their 'defensive' armament, which meant it didn't have to be stuck on afterwards. They were also built with sufficient accommodation for Service gunners. The Americans took a more pragmatic attitude to this side of things. They knew their ships were being built to go into the war zones and had no qualms about fitting guns to fire forward—most Liberty ships had a gun platform on the foc'stle, usually for an AA gun. Ships built to standard designs and dimensions must have been a great convenience to the military planners, who were responsible for the strategic loading of these ships when it came to preparing for the offensives that were to come.

So, after three years of war what armament did the merchant

ships have? It was in the area of anti-aircraft defences that most developments were made, and some of the early ones were rather strange.

To return to the early wartime voyages of the St. Merriel, you will remember the lone naval rating with the Lewis gun who we picked up in Scotland. When I finally left the ship she had been fitted with four plastic armoured machine gun nests, although the only guns we had were First World War Hotchkiss firing .303 shots, but even so this was an improvement. Gunnery courses were laid on at UK ports for merchant seamen volunteers.

On each side of the bridge, abaft the chart room, were positioned Hollman Projectors, which were absolute madness. The shot was a Mills Bomb, otherwise known as a hand grenade. A side lever is held in by a pin, which when withdrawn releases the lever (such as when the soldier hurls it at the enemy) and the bomb explodes in five seconds time. The projector was a vertical tube, loaded with an open tin can in which was a Mills Bomb with its pin removed and the lever held in by the sides of the can. It was fired vertically by compressed air or steam pressure and aimed or 'fired' by guesswork. In theory the can container fell away on launch, the bomb sailed up to 600 feet in the remaining seconds and exploded. It was reputed that they destroyed 12 aircraft! It's not said what else they destroyed—if the pressure was too low they had a reputation for shooting in the air for a short distance and falling back on board! On the Merriel we decided it was safer not to use them.

Positioned more or less alongside the Hollman Projectors were the 'Snowflakes', also vertical tubes but in this case each containing a rocket with a parachute flare, for illumination in the event of a night-time submarine attack. These were useful provided they were not fired accidentally.

Another similar 'funny' was called a P.A.C. (Parachute and Cable). Rocket propelled, it released a parachute dangling a length of wire, at the other end of which was a bomb. You can see the theory—a low flying aircraft approaches, at the appropriate time the weapon is fired, parachute opens, wire and bomb falls away, the aircraft obligingly flies into the wire, the parachute drags the wire and bomb up into the aircraft—bang! That's provided the thing has not got mixed up with the ship's whistle lanyard or wireless aerial on the way.

Twelve months later things had moved on. As a new Third Mate, I was making a tour of the ship to make myself familiar with things, when I came upon an army sergeant servicing a piece of apparatus on the bridge deck. It seemed to consist of two pieces of angle iron about five feet long, mounted almost vertically and which was obviously the 'launching rail' for a two inch rocket. Below was a cylindrical container, which I remember was about five inches in diameter and perhaps ten inches high, which had F.A.M. printed on its side. I said, "Hallo Sergeant, I haven't seen one of these before, what does F.A.M. mean?" Absolutely deadpan, he turned to me and said, "Fucking Awful Machine, Sir". (It really stood for 'Flying Air Missile'). When he described what it was supposed to do I had to agree, it was just a bigger and better (?) P.A.C.

Also on the bridge deck, on each side were the 'Pig Troughs', a much more dramatic weapon. The troughs, made of angle iron, held about twelve or fourteen two-inch rockets, each of which had a two-inch fused shell at its head, set if I remember correctly to explode at 750 yards. They were slung on gimbals so that they were always vertical. On the Monkey Island was the sight, which I thought was very ingenious and which relied upon an old coastal navigational ploy called 'doubling the angle on the bow'. One looked along the sight and waited for the aircraft to come on to the cross wire, then squeezed the trigger. The sight elevated upwards, one waited for the plane to come on to the cross wire again and squeezed the trigger a second time—this time the rockets went off—and how! Two dozen rockets fired simultaneously make a heck of a racket. One trough was just outside the radio office and the first time we fired them the Sparks on watch shot out ashen faced, thinking the worst—we agreed that in future he would be told in advance if we were likely to fire them.

A more sophisticated version of this previous static arrangement was the 'Pillar Box', a vertical cylindrical cabin or turret, in which sat the gunner who looked through a slot visor and open ring sights at the quarry—hence the nickname. On each side was a rack of twenty of the aforementioned rockets. By using hand-wheels, the gunner could rotate the turret and elevate the troughs, using the sights to lay them onto the target. Both sides could be fired together or separately, again dramatically and extremely noisily.

Occasionally, a ship would be fitted with the much-coveted Bofors anti-aircraft gun. This was an automatic cannon, firing 40mm calibre high explosive shells at around 100 rounds per minute, with an effective ceiling of around 13,000 feet.

The four plastic-armoured machine gun emplacements became standard, but were now fitted with the Oerliken 20mm cannon—much more re-assuring in its aggressiveness and loaded if I remember correctly with, in succession: solid shot, tracer incendiary and high explosive shell.

Of course, none of this was really lethal stuff, although it did have its successes. Its purpose was to lay a defensive barrage at about 2000 feet and if it put the pilot off his aim so that he missed, that was good enough. Against some pilots it certainly was effective, especially when a whole convoy erupted and some were put off altogether, but the more determined dived through it with apparent impunity.

All ships had a stern mounted surface firing gun, usually of about four-inch calibre and of First World War vintage or even earlier (See our training on the St. Merriel).

So who fired and looked after all this stuff? It was clearly now beyond the scope of 'Old Joe' and his few volunteers. I have already mentioned an army sergeant. By this time in addition to the RN DEMS (as in Defensively Armed Merchant Ships) gunners, there was also a Maritime Ack-Ack Regiment. I think they had volunteered, like the naval ratings, to serve with the DEMS. Ships at this time would have perhaps eight military personnel, both army and navy, with a senior n.c.o. in charge, maybe an army sergeant, a naval killick, or even a sergeant of marines. They seemed to get together, were well organised and conscientious, and did a good job. Although under the discipline of the ship's master, who delegated to one of the officers, they were not subjected to the same rigid stuff as in their parent service, which may have been a big attraction. Volunteer ship's personnel made up the numbers.

The USA, with its greater resources, provided its merchant ships with what seemed to us to be a greater number of naval personnel, aptly named the Armed Guard. Although the defence of their merchant ships still required a contribution from the merchant seamen 'volunteers', they were not so dependant upon them as we were.

13

DANGEROUS CARGO

Operation Torch and the Bone air raids

The telegram came. Bags packed, I said goodbye to Edna and slept one more night at Alvan before leaving for Cardiff. By this time I'd done the journey so many times I knew it by heart: through Wolverhampton, Birmingham, Worcester, Hereford, Abergavenny, Newport and finally arriving in Cardiff. I put my kit in the station left luggage office and went to the Pool office in dockland. There I was asked to join the Fort a la Corne, which was actually in Cardiff docks, and of course I knew what she would be like—so I had no qualms.

By the time I'd collected my kit and found my way to the ship it was early evening. All was quiet. Since these ships were virtually modern facsimiles of the St. Merriel, I knew my way around. Nobody was in the Second Mate's cabin so I knocked on the First Mate's door and a voice called, "Come in!" I entered—and there was a rather small cherubic faced man knitting a golliwog!

I introduced myself and said that I was a knitter too! He made me most welcome, said the Old Man was ashore and that the Second Mate who lived in Cardiff had gone home for the night. "Dump your kit in your cabin, bring your knitting and come and have a drink".

This we were doing when the Old Man came aboard looking for the Mate. He popped his head around the door, saw the two of us sitting knitting away and couldn't believe his eyes. "What the bloody hell sort of ship is this?" he exclaimed. Actually it was a very good ship—I think the happiest on which I sailed—but unfortunately this wasn't to last for long.

That was Captain R A Grove, a weathered, grey haired, heavily built over-weight individual who had spent his pre-war career in Eastern Waters and no doubt that was where he had learned to drink the hard stuff, by the bottle. I never saw him with more than he could carry, but that was quite a drop. I was fortunate to have Captain Grove as Master for my first trip as Third Mate. He had never met me before, but it was as though he assumed from the beginning that I knew what I had to do and that I would do it conscientiously. It must have required a lot of willpower to walk off the bridge and leave me, a twenty-year-old, in charge of his ship—especially in convoy at night-time. He was always courteous and never interfered. I think he probably spent some time walking the lower bridge out of sight, to see how I was coping with the station keeping, but that's jumping ahead.

In the morning I was able to have a look around and I was favourably impressed. The ship was brand new, having just been sailed over from Vancouver where she had been built. On the after bulkhead in the saloon was a plaque, which stated that Captain Louis-Francois la Corne had established Fort a la Corne in Saskatchewan, but when the French lost Montreal in 1760 he made his way back to France.

I don't think the British people at the time, or even later, were aware of what a great contribution the Canadians made to the Battle of the Atlantic in material and personnel.

I liked my cabin with its dark mahogany stained furniture. It was about eight or nine feet square, larger than anything I'd had before and I thought it quite spacious, although when Edna saw it later on she thought it claustrophobic! In addition to a bunk with drawers beneath there was a six foot settee, a wardrobe, a desk with club type upholstered chair and I immediately was aware that the porthole with cast iron deadlight was large enough to scramble through in an emergency. What's more, being a brand new ship there were no cockroaches! I also liked the saloon—which really was spacious. On the port side was a dining table large enough to seat the Old Man with all the deck and engineer officers together, plus the sparks—none of that nonsense about oil and water don't mix. To starboard were settees in the corners, small fixed tables with club chairs where one could write, study, relax or just play bridge

The bridge itself was well equipped too with Admiralty Aldis daylight signalling lamps, telescope and binoculars. There was a marvellous control box set up for the degaussing but it still had the old magnetic compasses. Very reassuring were the four steel lifeboats, one of them fitted with a four-cylinder engine. It would be one of my responsibilities to maintain them. One difference from the St. Merriel with these new ships was that the sailors & firemen lived aft in the poop, rather than under the forecastle head.

The Second Mate turned up during the morning. David Evans was, I would guess, about twenty-four, dark and handsome. I would think he had been brought up to the sea. His father was a Master Mariner and so had been his grandfather. I don't think David had served an apprenticeship; I think he had just gone to sea with his father when he was old enough, as had his brother and mother before the war. They had just recently recorded a programme for BBC Welsh Radio about the family who had all been shipwrecked at one time or another. His brother was in the RN. David had been torpedoed twice already, the last time on the tragic convoy PQ17, which we had passed on our way home coming back from Russia. For sailing his lifeboat of survivors to Murmansk and looking after them there, he had been awarded the MBE. He had great ability, a strong personality and was a natural leader—I thought he was great. The First Mate was quieter, a shrewd and capable individual and from the start we made a good team.

We signed on in the second week of November 1942, a crew almost entirely from South Wales and larger than I was used to.

The ship being a coal burner, we had nine or twelve firemen—three or four to a watch—and a contingent of ten DEMS gunners, making a compliment of a little over fifty. We went to the coal tips and took on ballast, which was levelled off and covered with wooden dunnage boards, then on to another quay to load military stores.

Allied troops had begun Operation Torch, the invasion of North Africa, so one did not need to be clairvoyant to guess where we were going. To me it was a repetition of the loading of the St. Clears, a procedure I was to become familiar with. The cargo comprised trucks, bren carriers, tanks, wireless wagons, stores, ammo': cleats were welded to the decks to facilitate the lashing down of cargo carried on deck. The difference this time was that right forward in number one hold we loaded cased petrol. These were rectangular four-gallon cans, two to a cardboard case (I think). Board of Trade regulations said that they should not be stacked more than five high, for fear that the weight of more layers would crush the lower cans, but this was wartime. How many layers we stacked I don't know, but it looked like half the height of the hold to me.

We had a routine passage out, meeting a convoy from Milford Haven going north up the Irish Sea and picking up other ships on the way, then heading westwards out into the Atlantic, before turning south and then eastwards towards the Straits of Gibraltar. I remember being impressed by the number and quality of the escort—destroyers as well as corvettes and a rescue trawler in the rear ranks! The occasional Catalina or Sunderland flying boat would be seen circling around—it all looked very business like.

We had never contemplated losing the war, although at times it was worrying because it was difficult to see how we could win. Now we could sense that times were changing. The Eighth Army was seeing off Rommel in the Western Desert and the First Army, whom we were to supply, was to join up with them. We were pleased to be part of it. Russia was stemming the tide at Stalingrad and the tremendous potential of the USA was coming on stream.

What we did not know was that Torch coincided with the start of a new Atlantic U-boat offensive. In order to escort our Torch convoys, involving hundreds of ships, the Atlantic convoys were denuded. In November, U-boats sank 117 Allied ships totalling 700,000 tons and another 100,000 tons were lost through other causes, the heaviest losses of the war. My luck was still holding.

Neither did we know that up until 1943 the German Navy would be able to read the Allied Convoy Cipher and therefore know the numbers, varieties, locations, departure dates and changes of directions of all Allied convoys. The Allies did not change to a totally secure cipher until November 1943.

I had no problems with the watch keeping. I had spent so much time on the bridge during the last two years of my apprenticeship that I was familiar with both the routine and the practicalities of station keeping. At the end of my night watch David would turn up on the bridge at about five minutes to midnight. We would chat, discussing the events of the day and the current situation for about fifteen minutes whilst his eyes adapted to the darkness, whereupon he would say, "Right-ho, I've got her". Then I would go into the chartroom to read the barometer. On the St. Merriel we had had an old mercury barometer a yard long slung in gimbals, complete with vernier. The new 'replacement' ships simply had an aneroid—it didn't seem anywhere near as nautical. I'd write up the log, wish David goodnight and head off to my bunk.

Watch keeping at night-time was quite tiring and I was always ready to 'drop off' when I got to my cabin. If the ship was rolling, I had a technique of bracing my knee against the bunk board with my back against the bulkhead and I'd drift off, lulled by the creaks and groans of the ship. Every ship creaks.

Occasionally, one or two of the escorts would make a swift foray to drop depth charges and sometimes the air escort could be seen doing the same, but we suffered no interference. Exploding depth charges made a significant metallic bang against the ship's hull and it was only courteous, as well as reassuring, to ring the engine room and let them know 'down below' what was happening.

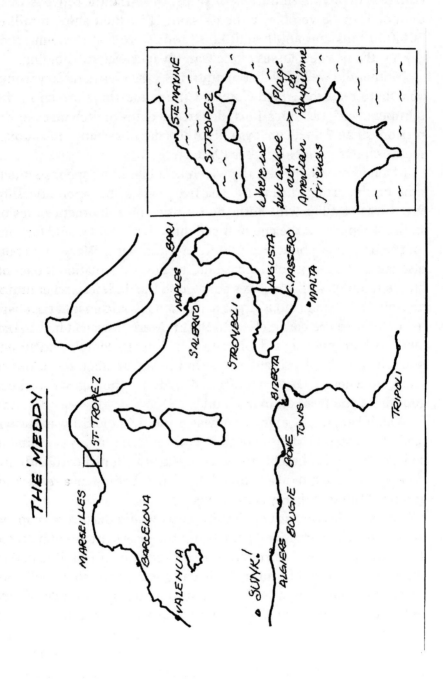

I think that first we anchored in some bay off Morocco and shortly after convoyed along to Oran. After a day or two we moved on to Algiers where we seemed to stick. There was a tremendous amount of shipping about. We began to get the impression that nobody wanted us and kept shoving us on to somewhere else. It became apparent afterwards that we were indeed part of a deliberate scheme of things. Our destination was Bone (now Annaba), which our airborne and commando forces had captured on November 12th and which was to become the main forward supply base for the 1st Army. We just had to wait and take our turn in the queue while the harbour was being cleared. Eventually we took convoy from Algiers, shedding ships at Bougie and Phillipeville and losing two ships to torpedoes on the way.

When we arrived at Bone things didn't look too reassuring. There was a small bay harbour, with a line of quays protected on the outer side from the open sea by a long mole. At the entrance was a small oil terminal, complete with a wrecked tanker. All was ablaze, billows of black smoke going skywards in daylight and dark reddish flames doing the same at night-time. We moored alongside the quay towards the far end, maybe a week or more before Christmas. The STO (Sea Transport Officer, usually an RNR lieutenant) came aboard to check us out and to arrange discharging procedure. This was to be done by a Docks Operating Company of the Royal Engineers, key figures of which were dockers in civvy life and members of the Pioneer Corps—the general humpers of the Army. We were warned to be on the alert for air raids at any time, the most usual time being around midday.

We hoisted derricks, stripped hatches, and next morning the army swarmed aboard. It was all very business like—they knew what they were doing. It all came to an abrupt halt approaching midday when we had the first air raid warning. Lying close to the inside of the mole on the seaward side of the harbour was a RN cruiser acting as guardship. She presumably had first contact on the radar, and hooted off her steam whistle as a warning. With that, all work stopped and the Pongoes took off ashore to whatever air raid shelters were available. Our gunners closed up at their stations and

I went up on Monkey Island to spot. The guardship began addressing the harbour over its tannoy, giving bearing and range—it was invariably seaward—and would occasionally fire a shell to give us a visual indication, since we could not always see the planes at this stage. To the east of the harbour were high hills and from first sighting the planes would circle to the east beyond them.

This was the tense waiting time with all eyes and gunsights on the crest of the hills. As the planes appeared, first the cruisers, destroyers and shore batteries opened up and when the planes began their dives the smaller stuff on our ship and all the others with a gun to bear joined in. The din was indescribable. I was petrified for a short period, with my legs turned to 'jelly', never having heard such a concentrated cacophony before, but I quickly recovered. In a few minutes it was over, score nil—nil, the bombs having gone into the harbour.

The squaddies returned, saying such things as, "Maybe that's it for today then" and started work again, the gunners checked their weapons and refilled magazines ready for the next time. It was from that time that I came to believe that if aircrews were determined enough, then nothing could stop them. It didn't seem possible that they could dive through all that flack and get away with it as they did. But they had missed! Perhaps they were not all that determined and perhaps it was the intensity of our fire that had put them off, but we were not always going to be successful.

Of course the cry went up, "Where's the bloody RAF?" We didn't know, only that they were not helping us. I have read since that heavy rains had turned the Allied North African airfields into mud and that our planes couldn't get off the ground, whereas the Axis planes were flying off hard runways in Sardinia. It was also stated that these aircraft were Junkers 88s and another account I have read said they were Stukas. However, I distinctly remember them as being single engined straight winged planes—either Me. 109s or Fw. 190s.

Towards the end of our stay there was one occasion, when in the immediate stillness following the bombers passing over, a lone plane was seen flying in a northerly direction between the hills and us. Every piece of small arms opened up on it. As it turned away towards the hills I saw its silhouette and called out, "I think it's a Spitfire!" Last seen, it was heading over the hills trailing smoke, an event summarised by one of our gunners as, "Serves t'bugger right, if he canna get here when he's needed he can piss off!"

Number one hold smelled ominously of petrol and when the 'tween deck hatch covers were removed it was overpowering, clearly a problem. 'No Smoking' notices went up, no army boots were allowed and all fire precautions that the army and we could muster were put in place. Those working in the hold soon began to suffer from nausea and had to be lifted out. Clearly there was petrol awash in the bottom of the hold from crushed tins. We had no facility to pump it out—petrol vapour in the ship's pipelines could be lethal. Nor could the army provide any solution.

To get out the tins that were intact, the technique finally used was for four squaddies in plimsolls to stand on the edges of a square wooden pallet and be craned into the hold. There they would stack as many cans as they could on to the tray in as short a time as possible—usually a couple of layers—and immediately be craned out before they succumbed, whereupon another group of four would take their place. They deserved medals.

I recently came across the book 'The Desert War' by Alan Moorhead, from which I quote the following paragraph. "The Germans designed what appears to be the best (petrol) container for the desert—flat, solidly built, holding five gallons—it could be used over and over again. (Known to us as a Jerry can) The great bulk of the British Army was forced to stick to the old flimsy four-gallon container. The majority was used only once. Thousands were smashed in transit and leaked entirely. We would put a couple of petrol cans in the back of the truck. Two hours of bumping over desert rocks usually produced a suspicious smell. Sure enough we would find that both our cans had leaked." It really was a criminal waste of a precious resource, and that included the lives of the tanker crews who transported the stuff in the first place.

Always, we had the midday air raid to look forward to. The odd bomb did fall ashore, but thank goodness not at our end, where the unloaded petrol cans were still stashed on the quayside—it could have been catastrophic. A disappointment to me was that since we were moored alongside and the ship was rigged for discharging the cargo, our sergeant gunner, who was closed up in the Pillar-Box, never had a clear field of fire and couldn't let fly his rockets.

After some days, a small convoy of four or five unloaded ships departed and their berths were taken up by new arrivals. What should tie up directly astern of us but the St. Merriel! Naturally I went aboard. Captain Owens was still in command, the first Mate Ellis was still with him as were the Chief Steward and the Swedish Bosun. I was excitedly made welcome; it was grand seeing them again.

There was no air raid on Christmas Day—everybody had a day off. We had a traditional dinner, but no one was in a celebratory mood— the toast was definitely wives and sweethearts. We had a young Sparks, only about seventeen years old, who may have been straight from school but was certainly straight from Yorkshire (William Hague could be a look alike). Because of his youth, overweight and general plumpness he was known as 'Porky', but Porky was no runaway; he was a dedicated Oerlikon gunner. Probably through inexperience, he imbibed unwisely and we had to put him in a bath of cold water to sober him up and keep him ready for action.

Somebody had the idea that we should go to midnight mass at the cathedral, which was in sight during daylight and within walking distance. This we did, but not being RC or even C of E, I could make nothing of it. I have since discovered that Bone, now Annaba, was in around 400 or so AD the seat of St. Augustine of Hippo, that leading theologian of the old Christian Church. I might then have looked at Bone a bit more curiously, had I known—or I might not have!

The next raid was on Boxing Day or the day following. Lying astern of the St. Merriel was the RN cruiser HMS Ajax of River Plate fame, probably acting in support of the guardship. The attacking planes carried only one bomb, so after they had swept across the harbour all went dramatically quiet and everyone looked around to take stock. On this occasion a couple of quayside buildings had gone up in a cloud of dust but nothing else seemed to have happened. Then Bennett, one of our two young apprentices, came running to the bridge calling, "Please Sir, they've dropped a bomb down the Ajax's funnel!" Bennett was a nice, well liked lad, but was also well known for his youthful enthusiastic exaggerations, so he got the immediate reply of, "Oh, go away!" or even ruder for his pains.

He was not far wrong. The bomb had gone through her deck plating at the base of the funnel and exploded below, causing quite a bit of damage. We heard that the armour belt had been cracked and there was concern that an engine room bulkhead might collapse. By this time we had almost completed discharging and our Old Man was able to offer them any of our dunnage boards which might be useful to shore up their engine room bulkhead, which they accepted with alacrity. We were proud to be able to help a ship we regarded with esteem.

We sailed just before the New Year of 1943, losing two ships to torpedoes just along the African coast on the way to Algiers. From there we took convoy home, which was quite uneventful, thank goodness—we still had about three feet of petrol washing about in the fore hold! When we got to the UK nobody wanted to receive us! No port would let us in until the petrol was cleaned out and we were 'gas free'. Eventually we anchored in the Mersey off Liverpool; the Fire Service brought out a lighter of some kind and with their own apparatus pumped us dry.

Then it was down to Newport in South Wales and all the Welshmen were happy. Since this was the port of return to the UK the ship would pay off there, even though the voyage had lasted only a little over two months. We officers got on so well together that we all agreed to sign on again for the next trip. As only five or six days leave was due, I decided that I would save mine up and if possible get Edna to come and stay on the ship for a while. The Old Man gave his permission and the Docks' Security Officer gave his, subject to an interview. As we were not married, she would not be able to sleep on board, but I was able to find for her bed and breakfast quite near to the dock gates.

Captain Groves was not the sort of man who kept his paper work up to date on a daily basis; he just waited until it was unavoidable.

In this case it meant working out the wages due to everybody on paying off day, taking into account what they had already drawn, what they had bought from the ships bond, what allotment they had made, National Insurance, pensions and tax. It was made known to me that I should assist and I reported to his day room at 8pm. He was at the organising stage and already half way down a bottle of Johnnie Walker. By midnight we were going well and he had started on the second bottle. There was no electronic gadgetry at that time, just ready reckoners, and of course it was all in pounds, shillings and pence, old money. We finished just after three in the morning, before the second bottle ended—he probably had what was left for a nightcap. I was just glad to get to bed.

I met Edna at the railway station. We went to see the port Army Security Officer who was sufficiently impressed to issue her with a docks pass and we walked to the ship. Whilst I had been away meeting Edna, the ship had needed to be moved a short distance and the accommodation ladder, which had non slip steps and a rope 'handrail', was not yet in place. The only way aboard was by climbing about twelve or fourteen feet up an ordinary ladder. To say she was taken aback at this would be an understatement. There was some resistance, but with encouragement from a number of the crew on board and me she intrepidly climbed up and was handed over the bulwarks. This was a good start—sailors like a girl with a bit of pluck!

It was not unusual for officers' wives to stay on board whilst ships were in the UK but I think Edna was the only female on board at that time. She occasioned that famous question by Captain Groves who, on catching a glimpse of her when he came aboard, went to the Mate's cabin and enquired, "Is that the Third Mate's Judy?" Having ascertained that it was, he conscientiously did his duty as Master of his ship and we were requested to go to his cabin for an evening drink. I had to take her to her 'digs' at the end of the day and meet her in the morning to take her back to the ship. What she thought of it all I don't know, I'm not sure whether she told me, but I know I was very proud to have her aboard.

During the week, David said that his parents were giving a party at their Cardiff home, to celebrate all the family being in the UK together at one time. Would we like to go if he could clear it with the Mate, since one of the deck officers always had to be aboard? The Mate said yes so we went, whether by bus or train I can't remember now. We were made most welcome. It was grand, not a static formal affair. All manner of friends and relatives turned up and departed at all sorts of times, staying for longer or shorter periods. We of course were relying on David's local knowledge of how to get back, but it wasn't up to date. When he thought it was time to leave it was discovered that the last transport had gone. That was not a problem and in no time they had solved the sleeping arrangements for us to stay overnight. Edna was just bewildered by the ease with which it was all done. I was a bit anxious on returning aboard as I had been de facto AWOL since midnight, but the Mate simply brushed it aside. It was that sort of a ship—we just worked together.

To refer once again to Porky, he had sent home for his portable gramophone, but before it arrived the Marconi Company took him off the ship and sent him elsewhere. The gramophone arrived, but with no records. Porky had gone we knew not where and there didn't seem to be the time nor the will to find out, so Edna and I slipped ashore and bought a record of the Tchaikovsky No. 1 Piano Concerto. It was not greeted with great enthusiasm. I remember when it was first played the saloon steward quite wrinkled his nose, but it was not long before he was winding up the machine and playing the first movement whilst he set the dining table. It was the only record we had and it got a fair hammering.

Edna had to go back home. Very soon afterwards she wrote to say that it had been found that she was suffering from anaemia. At that time she was working in a Darlaston factory, operating a lathe making very small screws for the Rolls Royce Merlin engine. In addition to prescribing 'iron tablets', the doctor had said that the working conditions were injurious to her health and that she should change her job. She did so and took employment in the personnel office at Rubery Owen. Marvellously, she had a boss who was not only kind to her but also had two sons who had trained as wireless operators and were in the Merchant Navy. Henceforth, taking her holiday when I was on leave would not be problem!

14

ABANDON SHIP!

The loss of the Fort a la Corne

We started to load the same type of military cargo as on the previous voyage, but this time there was no cased petrol! Sadly, the First Mate was taken from us and a new one named Williams arrived, a native of Newquay, Cardiganshire. It didn't take David long to establish that they had acquaintances in common, a characteristic of the Welsh. He was a smallish man of about forty I suppose, a typical Welshman, one of the trilby hat brigade and a chapel man who did not drink alcohol or swear, but who always had a hand rolled cigarette. His initials were WT and I immediately christened him 'Watertight Williams', not to his face at this stage, but when we knew him better and David told him he thought it a great compliment. He was very capable in an unobtrusive sort of way and we continued to work well together.

The first part of the voyage was a repeat of the previous one, but as soon as we swung out into the Atlantic we ran into the most severe stormy weather for many a year. Very quickly ships had no option but to heave to and ride it out as well as they were able, neglecting or ignoring the convoy. The Fort a la Corne performed very well. With just sufficient engine revolutions to keep steerageway, the wind fine on the starboard bow, greyness everywhere and visibility almost nil with constant rainsqualls, we pitched, banged and buffeted our way along.

I don't think the Old Man left the bridge for three days. Occasionally he would say, "I'll just have a kip on the chartroom settee, call me if necessary" and in half an hour he would be back, peering over the bridge 'dodger'. As David used to say, "With his hand in his pocket scratching his balls"—I'd never noticed this until David pointed it out to me. The hours of darkness were the worst; somewhere out there were forty or so other ships all in the same predicament—where and how near were they? It was a relief to go below, knowing that David was up there on watch.

The distance we travelled through the water was measured in those days by a ship's 'patent log'. This was a clock-like device actuated by an elongated propeller, which was towed through the water on the end of a cord 'log line', usually but not always over the stern. They were surprisingly accurate. (Nothing to do with the written log which was a record of events). When one wanted to know the distance travelled, one whistled for the standby man who went aft to 'read' it. Under our storm conditions though, it was hardly moving through the water and just hung downwards at an angle of about forty-five degrees doing nothing useful at all. Navigation was now just guesswork, or perhaps one should say estimation based on years of experience. At noon some sort of positional fix was necessary, so the Old Man and David would look over the side of the bridge at the water, and the Old Man would say, "What shall we give her today, fifty?" David would concur and fifty sea miles would be marked off on the chart from the last position.

One morning the Bosun came up on the bridge to say that some heavy thuds could be heard coming from number four hold. The Mate, David, the Bosun and the watchmen opened up the hatch to find that a bren carrier had broken adrift and with the rolling of the ship it was doing its best to smash up everything in its vicinity. They managed to capture and secure it before too much damage was done.

Next morning on my watch the sky seemed a bit lighter but the sea was still very rough. David came up to relieve me for breakfast, going into the chartroom first to read the logbook and barometer. He had a collection of rhyming couplets relating to sea and weather lore, which I suppose he had learned from his father—I wish I could remember them. On this occasion, he said the glass was up a bit. He thought in an hour or so the horizon would begin to lighten on the starboard bow and the wind would back a point or two—then he quoted one of his jingles. He was correct of course and it began to clear.

That afternoon David was on watch, with the Old Man still on the bridge, when an escort destroyer came up on the port quarter, leaping like a gazelle from wave crest to wave crest in showers of spray. She switched on her loudhailer and called, "Good afternoon Captain, is all well?" On being assured that it was, he switched on again and said that the Commodore was off to our port on such and such a bearing, just a few miles away, and would we close up as convenient. It seemed amazing to me that in just a few days almost the whole of the convoy was back together again. I suppose we had all been doing the same thing and we were never very far apart, it was just that we couldn't see each other. A few ships found their own way to Gibraltar and none was lost.

As before, we went first to Algiers and again we had to wait our turn for a convoy to Bone. Edna had told me that her brother Bill, a postmaster in civvy street, was with the Army Post Office in Algiers, a case for once of a round peg in a round hole! I got a day off and went in search of him. It was surprisingly easy—all the army types seemed to have some idea where their post office was and by early afternoon I had found his billet. We had a couple of hours' chat and tea, whereupon it was time to return. I had not met him before, nor have I since, although Edna insists that I have!

Bone had changed: there was no longer a fire at the oil terminal, the wrecked tanker had gone and so had the derelict buildings. At the far corner of the square, an enterprising Frenchman had set up a wine bar where one could sit outside in the sunshine with a glass of the local vin rouge, his trade considerably enhanced by the possibility of chatting up his attractive but chaste daughter.

We had previously left there at the end of 1942 and I would have looked at Bone and its harbour more closely on our return if I had known then what I discovered only last year. This is a quote from John Slader's 'The Fourth Service': "North African ports like Bone were the main supply base for the First Army, virtually on the front line and suffering almost incessant air attacks. Each convoy had to be fought through. On New Year's Day 1943 the Novelist and Harpalyce were both damaged, the day after the St. Merriel and the new tanker Empire Metal were destroyed". (A fuller account by Captain Owens can be read in P M Heaton's book on the Saint Line). I'm glad I didn't know about what had happened to the St. Merriel at the time and if there was any wreckage still there I don't remember it. Neither do I remember any of us going ashore except to the bar. I suppose there must have been a sizeable city to explore because it had a Cathedral, but the only thought we had was to unload the cargo and get away. We would soon have enough excitement of our own.

We left Bone in Convoy ET16. I cannot remember now, whether on our voyage westwards we called in to Algiers to collect a new convoy or whether ships came out from Algiers to join us, but I think it was the latter. That evening, on our way along the North African coast, David and I were sitting in my cabin having a chat before he turned in and I went on watch. Through the open porthole came the distant whoop-whoop, whoop-whoop of the siren from one of the portside escorts. Ever on the alert, David said, "What's that?" and immediately dashed out and up the ladder to the bridge. I followed him out, but turned the other way with the intention of seeing whether the Commodore was flying any signal.

I had taken not more than three or four steps when there was the most almighty bang beneath me, which threw me off my feet and on to my backside, followed by a downpour of sea water and showers of plastic armour splinters from the machine gun nests above. The ship heeled to starboard and slowed, as though she had run on to a sandbank. I hung on to the cleats of number three hatch combing until the deluge had finished—I had visions of it washing me overboard—and then got to my feet. Immediately another explosion occurred and the same thing happened once again. I remember I was quite furious at the injustice of it, it seemed so unreasonable for this to happen twice. This second time I let myself be washed under the bridge accommodation ladder, which I hung on to, so that I could get some protection from the falling debris.

Of course I realised what had happened. There had been attacks in the same place on two previous occasions and this time it was our turn to be hit, together with another ship. (I have since discovered this was the Norwegian MT Hallanger).

My first thought was, "Lifejacket and panic bag", both of which where in my cabin, but entry into the accommodation was now impossible—doors were off and lying at all angles, wrecked furniture was all over the place and shattered plastic flooring was everywhere. My second thought was to get up to the bridge for orders. The amidships was already sinking and I could see the bows rising in front of me with the terrible distressing sound of tearing metal. As I got to the top of the first ladder I met the bridge party coming down—the Old Man, the Mate, David, an apprentice and a few others. The order was, "Abandon ship!"

My lifeboat was the port side forward, the Mate's was port side aft, but neither of them was there, they had been thrown somewhere by the blast of the explosions. David's boat on the starboard side could not be lowered because the ship's plates had been blown out underneath it. That just left the Old Man's boat, which fortunately was one of the larger ones. By this time the Bosun was up on the boat deck with some of the experienced men, clearing it away and lowering it.

David, always the man of action, called to me, "Come on, we'll launch the after rafts", and that's what we did. It was at this stage that I realised for the first time how calm the sea was, it was like the proverbial millpond. David and a couple of the sailors went down the rope ladder to one of the rafts. I looked forward and saw that the lifeboat was still alongside, holding on by the painter and that there was still standing room, so I tottered forward and to cries of, "Come on, Third!" I was helped in. The amidships of the Fort a la Corne was by then so low in the water that I just stepped off it into the lifeboat, no ladder was necessary.

There was Watertight Williams, sitting in the stern sheets with the tiller under his arm, showing no more concern than if it had been a boat drill, with just enough steerage way maintained to enable him to keep the boat from banging against the ship's side, whilst waiting to see if anyone else would turn up.

The Third Engineer arrived. As he was going to go on watch later at midnight, he had turned in early. No longer a young man, he wore dentures and was bald on top. Rudely awakened, he had rapidly thrown on some clothes and in his dash from the cabin had, he thought, picked up something useful. It transpired that he had grabbed his hairbrush and left behind his dentures—he could see the funny side of this!

Then came the Second Sparks, an Irish lad of about eighteen and in rather a panic. He didn't wait for the boat to come alongside. Thinking he was being left behind, he jumped into the sea and made an energetic crawl stroke for the boat, calling, "Wait for me, I can't swim!" but he certainly could. Being due on the midnight watch, he had also turned in and unable to get through the wrecked accommodation he had had to clamber out through a porthole.

When it was apparent that no one else was going to arrive, someone cut the painter and we sheered off. There, not more than half a cable away, was one of the two rescue trawlers from the convoy. These ships were one of the reorganisation measures brought in by Admiral Max Horton, an ex submariner who became C in C of Western Approaches and who was the right man for the job. They were more than maids of mercy; the shortage of seamen was as serious as the shortage of ships. Often converted trawlers, but sometimes small passenger boats, they were RN manned and carried emergency food, clothing and first aid. Although not active as escorts, they were fitted with HF/DF equipment and kept watch for U-boat transmissions. It was a great boost to our morale to see one or two of these ships at the tail end of the convoy.

Somehow, a couple of oars were shipped and we paddled over to the trawler. There must have been about forty-five of us and it was standing room only with about six inches of freeboard. Helping hands soon had us on board and then the skipper turned towards the raft. By then the sun had gone down. One of my abiding memories is the silhouette of the raft in the foreground and against the red sky of the sunset in the distance was the broken backed ship—a classic image of a shipwreck at sea.

With all on board the trawler a count was made. The first attempt brought a tally of one too many, so we split up into our departments and tried again. The solution: thirteen firemen instead of twelve, one of them being an army deserter who had stowed away, no doubt with the connivance of the stokers. The poor fellow had picked the wrong ship. The Fort a la Corne sank in about twenty minutes.

By then I had a bit of a headache and felt 'whoosy', maybe I had a touch of concussion or shock or both and the trawler skipper sent me to lie down for a while on his cabin settee. An hour or so later I felt better and went out on deck in the dusk to see that we were already up with the convoy. Someone took me to see our crew. They were sitting or lying sprawled all over the mess deck—provided with fags and cocoa, they were content. As someone said, "If we had to be torpedoed, it couldn't have been better." My luck was still holding.

Next day, to ease the crowding on the trawler, we were split up between some of the escorts. I took a dozen men aboard a Hunt class destroyer, the name of which I very much regret that I have forgotten, particularly as she was one of those which took a very spirited part in the defence of Bone harbour. They made us very welcome. The 'Doc' said he had better have a look at the bash on my forehead and took me down to his hospital.

It was then that I realised what a scruffy lot we looked. I was unwashed, unshaven, wearing salt stained old gear, one eyebrow thick with dried blood—some of which had run down and stained the collar of my shirt—the only bit of uniform I was wearing was the original pair of trousers from the Liverpool Sailors Home outfitters. My pullover was one that I had knitted myself out of khaki wool from some unravelled 'comforts' and since there wasn't enough of that I had incorporated a broad green horizontal stripe across the chest. In that state, I lay on his immaculate white operating table whilst he investigated my 'wound'. Having cleaned it up, his verdict was that it was a nice clean cut caused by the sharp edge of a plastic splinter and because it had been well washed in seawater it was healing nicely. He thought it was as well to leave it alone, and so it proved.

I spent the morning cleaning myself up as well as I could and was introduced to the Commander and his officers. They were, I suppose, a typical wartime mix of RN, RNR and RNVR. The navigator or 'pilot' was ex Merchant Service. The Captain was in his mid thirties: very much the king of his castle, he seemed to be well liked and respected. I slept in his cabin; he had another bed elsewhere. Talking to him about losing two more ships in more or less the same place as previous attacks, he said that the Meddy was not a good place for Asdic contacts because of the various layers of salinity. Where we had been sunk was particularly bad—it was difficult to get a good 'ping'—and so was a good place for a U-boat to lie in wait. He called over a young sub-lieutenant RN and told him to take me down to the Asdic room so that I could hear for myself. I could tell how difficult it must be for them. From then on the 'subby' became quite friendly and took me under his wing, showing me around.

After a couple of days Gibraltar showed up on the horizon. We broke away from the convoy, the Old Man 'put her arse down' and we sped for the Rock at twenty-seven knots. I'd never been anywhere near that speed over the water before. It was quite a thrill to stand on the open bridge of the destroyer, with sheets of spray flying past. I was sad to leave this ship—there is a bond between seamen created by their affinity for the sea—but it was good to meet up with our old crew again.

For David, this had been his third sinking and the advantage of being with a man of experience is that he knows what to do next. "Never mind anything else," he said. "The first thing we have to do, when we get money, is to send a telegram home to say all is well, so that it gets there before the official telegram which starts, 'We regret to inform you …' " We were taken to some office to register, were given a small amount of money and then we sent our telegrams.

We were now officially DBS—'Distressed British Seamen'. You can see in my Discharge Book the entry, "Discharged at Sea. 30 March 1943". That is when we were sunk so that's when the voyage ended. In peacetime and for a while after the war started, so did the wages too and there arose the ridiculous situation whereby women married to seamen lost their allotment pay on the same day that their husbands lost their ship. That had eventually changed after protests and we received our pay from somewhere until we got home and went on leave.

Gibraltar had at one time a poor reputation for the indifferent way it treated survivors, but by the time of our arrival things were better organised and we couldn't complain. We were lodged in one of the main street hotels, not luxurious, but other naval and army officers were there, and then we were kitted out at a 'gents outfitters'. This was really a small clothing warehouse run by an enterprising Gibraltarian who had seen an 'opening in the market'. We were allowed one pair of shoes, two pairs of socks and underwear, two shirts, a tie, razor, suit, a few handkerchiefs and a small suitcase. Clearly other people had passed through before us, as there was not much choice in suits and the only one anywhere near my size was sugar bag blue in colour. All we could do then was to write letters home and wait.

We had sustained only two casualties: one of the apprentices had a fractured leg and the Old Man suffered a fractured pelvis. Whilst a lightweight like me was thrown into the air, Tubby Groves had more inertia. We went to see him in hospital, where he was in fine form as well as plaster from thighs to his chest. He said it itched like hell and in an aside to me David said, "He always was a good scratcher". Then of course there was the fate of the stowaway. I'm afraid there had been a posse of Military Police to escort him ashore.

We were not the only people who had been in trouble. March 1943 saw the start of a new U-boat offensive and the great convoy battles of the Atlantic. In that month U-boats operating in the Atlantic, Mediterranean, Arctic and Indian Oceans sank 105 ships totalling 590,000 tons, for the loss of sixteen U-boats. It was a success not to be repeated. With our American and Canadian Allies the tide slowly turned in our favour. April was evenly balanced but thereafter it was the U-boats that were taking unsustainable losses—although still around they had lost the major battle.

There was not much to do in Gib. We watched inter service football matches, famous for being played in plimsolls on a concrete pitch, saw the changing of the guard at the Governor's Palace, walked up the Rock and waited. I thought the best sight was from the water front, watching the aircraft taking off from the runway directly over the water, or watching the Sunderland and Catalina flying boats taking off and landing, especially if there was a bit of a chop.

I was the first to get away with a small party on a Polish cargo-passenger ship called the Lwow. I have to say I felt slightly anxious as we steamed out and formed up in convoy. I made sure I knew my way from the cabin to the boats and that my lifejacket was always handy. On the Fort a La Corne I had always taken my life jacket and panic bag up to the bridge with me when on watch and in the end I had been caught without them.

Apart from a bit of depth charging by the escort, we had a clear run home and I think we went to Liverpool. I know I arrived at

Wolverhampton railway station early in the morning before the trolley buses were running and walked home in my sugar bag blue survivor's suit. I had little luggage to carry!

I was given a month 'survivors leave' and as a Third Mate received £60 and an allowance of clothing coupons to re-kit. Fortunately there was an Austin Reed shop in Wolverhampton—a good quality national gents' outfitters in those days—which was able to supply the uniform and other necessities. I also bought a new civvy suit, as the survivor's issue was too much of an embarrassment. There was no profit in being shipwrecked. It didn't take long to spend £60 and I still had to get a new sextant, tables and textbooks. I remember that Edna was most chagrined that four pairs of long white oiled-wool seaboot stockings, which I had saved up from 'comforts' issues and from which she was going to knit me a roll neck sweater, had gone to the bottom.

What we did during those leaves is now a blur. Edna was able to get a few days off from work, but it sometimes meant working over on other occasions to make up for it. If the weather was reasonable there were parks we could visit during the daytime. There was the cinema, theatres at Walsall or Wolverhampton, there were still touring companies performing operas and perhaps an orchestral concert. It didn't really matter as long as we had time together—preferably just the two of us.

My time aboard the Forte a la Corne had been four months and nineteen days, but now she was lost.

47. *Military stores being off-loaded from a merchantman alongside at Bone. IWM. A 13810*

The next 9 Imperial War Museum pictures were taken I suppose by an official photographer. They are of various events at a number of invasion beaches but these procedures are typical and took place at all locations. Some were calmer and more peaceful than others!

48. *RE's in a merchantman's hold beginning to off load it's cargo. Note the rolls of steel mesh for stabilising roadways across the sands.*
IWM A 24506

49. Lowering a US vehicle and gun into a British landing craft – North Africa. IWM. A 12685.

50. A British gun and equipment going into what appears to be a US landing craft – anxiously watched by the men on the deck of the ship. IWM. E 8161.

51. *Supplies from a liberty ship going into an American DUKW at their landing beach in Sicily. IWM. NA 5320.*

52. *Supplies being offloaded into a British DUKW – there seems to be a queue! Italy. IWM. NA 12142*

53. *A loaded DUKW drives ashore at Salerno. Note the road way across the sand 'paved' with wire mesh. IWM. NA 6636.*

54. *A convoy heading for the South of France. I wonder if the island in the background is where we anchored? IWM. A 25271.*

55. *A photograph from a British mine sweeper of swept mines exploding off the South of France. IWM. A 25223.*

56. *Landing craft heading for the South of France beaches and passing the US Control Ship. A bombarding battleship in the distance. IWM. A 25225*

57. Wedding Day.

58. Edna on our honeymoon.

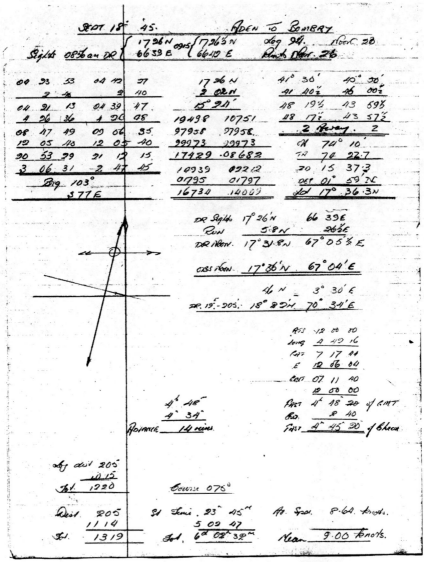

59. *Extract from my Atheltarn Sights Book for September 18th. 1945 on the leg Aden to Bombay. The sun sights were taken by sextant at 0845 local time to give the longitude position line. The true latitude and longitude was established precisely at the noon sights when the sun was at its highest. The distance covered (1319 nautical miles) and steaming time (6 days 2 hrs. 32 mins) since leaving Aden are shown below. Average speed was 9.00 knots.*

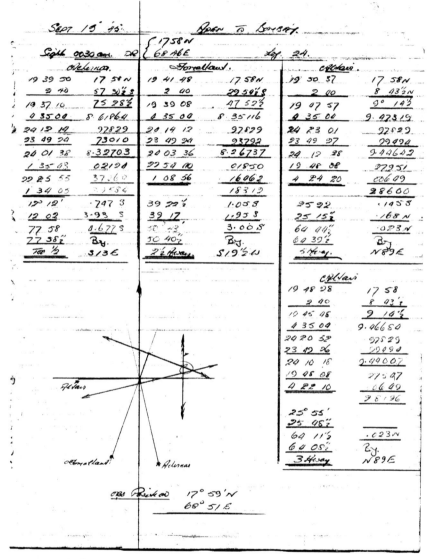

60. *Atheltarn Sights Book extract for nightime on Sep.19th.1945*
Why I was taking star sights at 30 minutes past midnight I don't know –
just to pass the time in the graveyard watch I should guess and probably
acknowledge a wonderfully clear night with a well defined horizon.

61. A page of entries in my discharge book.

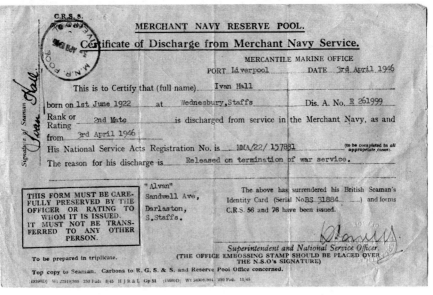

62. The Merchant Navy Discharge Certificate.

15

THE SICILIAN INVASION, SALERNO BEACHHEAD AND BARI

The Fort Walsh plies the Mediterranean

A month's 'survivors leave' might seem like a long time but it quickly passes and soon the call came to report to the Pool in Liverpool. When I got there I was told to join the Fort Walsh at Glasgow. You might well ask why I wasn't told to go to Glasgow in the first place but things didn't work like that. I went back to Lime Street Station and ascertained that there was a through train to Glasgow departing at eight o'clock in the evening. I bought my ticket and decided to buy a new sextant (which I still have) and to get something to eat.

At about half past seven I retrieved my kit from the left luggage office and went to the platform. The train was already standing there packed full of soldiery. I left my luggage on the platform and walked the length of the train—I just couldn't see how it was possible to get on, even the corridors were full. As I was walking back from the front end I saw a sleeping car attendant on the platform and in a flash of inspiration I asked if he had any spare berths. "Yes sir", he said. "Just one". Maybe he said that to everybody, but no matter, I slipped him a ten-bob note with the instruction, "Hold it, I'll be back with you in a minute". I collected my kit, handed it in to his care, paid up the difference in fare and as the train rattled out of Liverpool heading north I turned in, to be awakened in the early morning with a cup of tea as we steamed into Glasgow. It was the best rail journey I ever made and it was on the eve of my twenty-first birthday.

On the first of June 1943, my twenty-first birthday, I signed on as Third Mate on the Fort Walsh, which like my previous ship had just come over from Canada. She was managed by the Larinaga Shipping Co. of Liverpool. Famous as a long established British tramp ship company, this enterprise had been founded in 1864 by one Ramon de Larinaga, a Basque from Bilbao. The company had survived through the lean times of the Thirties slump and it still survived until the 1970's, when it was the last privately owned tramp company operating out of Liverpool. I remember the pre-war ships, which had yellow coloured masts and funnels, with two red bands round the funnel just like the Spanish flag. The ships always looked as though they were worked hard and could do with a coat of paint. I have learned since that during the war they managed nineteen 'Ministry' ships—Forts, Oceans and Empires—nine of which were lost. Fortunately, not the one I was sent to.

The Fort Walsh turned out to be a bit dull after the a la Corne. The Chief Steward of the Walsh was a Spaniard, a veteran company's man, but the only character I remember by name was the Second Mate and that for a strange reason, which I'll mention later.

A day or two later I was told she was going to be fitted with anti-torpedo nets. She already had the booms in place on the fore and main masts as I think most Fort boats did, but the nets had not been rigged. How effective they were I don't know but having already lost one ship through torpedoes I could only approve.

The fitting was to be done at night time and as I was the junior officer it was up to me to 'keep the deck'. There was nothing strange about that. What was strange was that I was told they were to be fitted by WRNS! One's vision of a WRN at that time was of a nice looking well spoken shapely lass in a white blouse, navy blue skirt and black stockings. It seemed an attractive responsibility but the vision did not seem to fit in with heaving around wire ropes and hauling steel nets to the tops of booms.

I need not have worried. When the young ladies came aboard they were WRNS I had never seen before,—young amazons clad in wellies and boiler suits well padded with jerseys, they had obviously been recruited for the job and knew what they had to do. Any thoughts of dalliance in the darkness or lighthearted flirtations disappeared immediately.

Actually we only streamed the nets once and that was in convoy in the Meddy on the way back to Gib for a convoy home. I have realised since that was the area where we lost the Fort a la Corne.

Having signed on the new crew, we moved from the Glasgow docks where the ship had discharged, anchoring off the small military port of Faslane in the Gare Loch. We waited there for some days until a berth became available (Faslane later became well known as the nuclear submarine base). It seemed to be in the middle of nowhere and it rained and rained and rained. Apart from the job in hand there was nothing to do, nowhere to go and nothing to see except damp greyness. The task was the same as before, to oversee the loading of another military cargo, much the same as on previous occasions

Security was tighter and we were told that the censor was strict. One had to write home, but what about? We couldn't say what we were doing; we couldn't say where we were or where we were going—not that we knew. The only thing to write about was the weather, and that was just cause for complaint! Writing paper was in short supply in those days and one wrote on both sides. When later on in the voyage I got a letter from Edna, it was to say that the letters she had received were unreadable, since they were full of holes. She showed them to me when I got home. Every reference to the weather had been cut out, literally, and with having to write on both sides, you can imagine the result.

In addition to the usual stuff, this time we loaded quite a number of DUKWs (four wheel drive amphibious trucks) and two LCTs (landing craft tank). The latter were placed on number two hatch where we had a 25-ton lift jumbo derrick—this ship was a multiple birth sister of the a la Corne. That raised some questions! What was the purpose of the amphibious vehicles and landing craft and where were we taking them?

Having completed loading, we swung compasses and then anchored somewhere in the upper reaches of the Clyde, along with many other ships, all similarly loaded. The weather improved. Then came another surprise—we were to hold lifeboat drill and whilst the crew were at their stations, service type gas masks were to be issued. We, the officers, had to see that everyone knew how to fit one. The check as to whether it was fitted correctly was to double the breathing pipe and grip it tightly, then to ask the wearer, "Can you breathe?" If they indicated that they could not, then there was no leak and it was a good fit.

For this voyage we had signed on Arab firemen; I think they were Somalis. You may wonder what Somalis were doing on a British ship that was quite clearly going into a war zone. I wonder myself, and I don't think it was out of enthusiasm for the British cause, it must have been solely for the money, but at that time we were glad to have them. They were on the whole quite young men, with a few older and more experienced amongst them, and their knowledge of English was scanty. I had three or four of them in my lifeboat and their attempts to put on the masks would have been quite hilarious if it had been a laughing matter. One young fellow did not have his fitting under his chin properly, so I adjusted it and went through the routine. "Can you breathe?" He nodded his head, so I squeezed tighter and asked again. No matter what I did he always nodded his head. Clearly something was wrong, so I took off the mask to examine it and found that the poor chap was nearly asphyxiated—he was gasping like a fish out of water. He thought that he should have been able to breathe during the test and hadn't wanted to offend me.

One of the chores I had was to type out crew lists every so often for the Old Man (we didn't have duplicating machines) and for the first time I became aware of, what were to me, the strange names of our Eastern brethren. I had to identify the various crewmembers from this list, but it was difficult since many of them seemed to have similar names but in a different order, usually interspersed with 'Bin' or 'Hadji'. One of them who spoke English then explained that these words were not names, but that Bin meant 'son of' and Hadji was a title meaning 'someone who has been on a pilgrimage to Mecca'.

Whilst we were moored there, we received a signal to say that Admiral Vian was coming aboard to 'inspect' us. That was very strange, as admirals might inspect naval ships but not merchantmen. However, I was quite keen to see this man, as we all were, for it was he who as Captain of the destroyer Cossack rescued some three hundred of our fellow seamen from the German prison ship Altmark in a Norwegian Fjord. We didn't put on our 'number ones', but we made sure we were presentable and stood in line in order of importance, and then with the appropriate flourishes he arrived in his Admiral's barge. As the Admiral who was in charge of operation 'Anvil-Husky' he knew where we would be going. We didn't and this visit, although soon over, was meant as a morale booster for us. He just took a quick look around and then departed with his entourage. Vian had the reputation of being a hard man and he looked it!

The big question that the joint planners had had to resolve, once the Axis Powers were removed from Africa, was "Where next?" The options were Sicily, Italy, the South of France or the eastern end of the Meddy. We guessed we were going to find the answer for ourselves.

Eventually, we all weighed anchor and streamed down the Clyde in a long gaggle, number pennants flying. The rain had stopped, the water was smooth, and the sun was shining—a fine summer's day with the Old Man and myself on the bridge. I spotted something ahead, just fine on the starboard bow and put the telescope on it. I couldn't quite make it out, but called to the Old Man that there was something odd out there—it looked like a man walking on the water, which provoked the immediate response of "Jesus Christ!" It was not until the 'thing' passed close by on a reciprocal course that we could see it was a miniature submarine, the skipper standing more or less with his feet awash and his back to the periscope. We didn't know it then of course, but in January the RN had taken delivery of six 'X' craft and what we saw was one of them on exercise. In September three of them would make a partially successful attack on the battleship Tirpitz in a Norwegian fjord.

We left the sheltered waters of the Clyde on June 25th 1943, formed up into convoy KMS19 and set off around the north of Ireland. The ocean escort came out from Londonderry to meet us and we made our usual wide sweep out into the North Atlantic before heading southwards. We had the feeling that the submarine menace was not what it had been and we now had many aircraft patrolling round the convoys.

Nevertheless, I thought it prudent to ask the Bosun for a piece of white cotton canvas and I stitched myself another panic bag. You will remember I lost the last one I had on the Fort a la Corne. If you wonder what it was like, it was a small canvas satchel with a shoulder strap, the intention being to pack in it a few valuable and useful items to take to the boat if one had to abandon ship. In mine, on the a la Corne, I had packed a spare pair of trousers, shirt, pants, socks and in an oilskin wallet some tobacco, cigarette papers (I rolled my own in those days), matches, a little money and a small photograph of Edna. That was to be repeated with the new one. Fortunately it was never needed for its proper function although after the war I would sling it over my shoulder as a satchel when riding my old Norton motor cycle. When at sea I, like many others, had long ago given up sleeping in pyjamas and at bed time changed into clean underwear, shirt, socks, an old pair of flannel trousers and a jersey if it was cool enough.

As we turned eastwards to head for the Gibraltar Straits the Focke Wolfe Condors found us, but they were reconnaissance or 'stooge' machines and made no attempt to attack. One afternoon we had both a Condor and a RAF Sunderland circling the convoy at the same time. On the far side of the convoy the Sunderland got belligerent and flew towards the Condor. We heard a rattle and saw some flashes of machine gun fire, causing the Condor to seek refuge by flying low close to the sea, whereupon the Sunderland flew directly above it and dropped either bombs or depth charges—we saw the splashes. The Condor took the hint and cleared off. Well done the Raff!

We had passed through the Straits and in the northerly distance just above the horizon could be seen the snow covered peaks of the

Sierra Nevada. Soon afterwards we heard the news that an Allied landing had been made on the southeast corner of Sicily. Now we knew where we were going.

Our beach turned out to be just north of Cape Passero in the southeast corner of the island and we anchored off shore on July 13th in what turned out to be a quite open roadstead. With the aid of the jumbo derrick we manoeuvred the landing craft over the side and into the water, followed by the numerous DUKWs. Other merchant ships arrived and began discharging too.

It was at that time the greatest seaborne force ever embarked. The invasion was successful of course, but it must have warned the planning 'executives' that there was an awful lot to learn. There had been a spell of bad weather and in poor visibility flights of glider-borne troops had been cast off over the sea by inexperienced 'tugs' and the men had drowned. Parachute troops were dropped miles from their targets yet proved to be a disruptive element to the enemy wherever they landed. However, the storming of the beaches had been successful, numbers were on our side and when we arrived on D+3 the beaches were quiet.

One or two RN cruisers and a WW1 monitor were drifting around the anchorage, giving support fire to order at distant targets. It was to me quite fascinating to see how, when it was fired, a broadside of the main armament caused a cruiser to move sideways in the water. What's more, if one happened to be in the right place behind the monitor, one could catch a glimpse of the fifteen-inch shells as they flashed in the sunlight when they turned at the top of their trajectory.

We had complete air supremacy, thank goodness, for the discharging was quite a shambles. The recommended technique was to hang a hefty mooring rope in a loop over each side, fastened to our mooring bits fore and aft. In theory, the landing craft and DUKWs were to make fast to these whilst the cargo was lowered into them. This may have worked when the troops trained in smooth water, but in our roadstead with a five foot swell running, it was beyond their capabilities to make fast.

For the landing craft things were not too bad: their weight made them fairly stable and once we had got their crews to ignore the side rope and make fast directly on to the ship things got better. Even so, it was difficult to hold them still long enough to place the large army trucks into them, there being no room to spare. The DUKWs were the real problem: they bounced around all over the place, while some of their crews did not have very good sea-legs and had no idea how to make a hitch to the side rope. Often, we would get a sling of stores or ammo' over their deck hatch and just as we were about to lower it in the craft would go adrift. It was remarkable we didn't have an accident.

The Second Mate and Sparks decided to go ashore with one of the craft to take a look around. They were back almost immediately. They said the way off the beach was marked with white tape, while scattered round and about were wrecked and overturned vehicles with notices saying 'Beware of Mines'. They came straight back to the safety of the ship.

Over the next few days the swell settled down, people became more expert and confident at their tasks and we got everything away. We too got away. Around the corner to the west of us, the Americans had their own bit of beach-head and the two prima donnas of that and future campaigns, Generals Patton and Montgomery, began to give voice. It was all rather sad and unnecessary.

We headed south to Tripoli on the north coast of Libya where we loaded Eighth Army military ware, much the same as before but with no landing craft. From there we went north to what was the shipping equivalent of Crewe junction—Augusta on the east coast of Sicily, between Catania and Syracuse. My memory is of a large bay anchorage that seemed to be right under Mount Etna, but looking at the atlas today I see that the latter is at least forty miles away. The bay could hold a great deal of shipping and was well curtained off with anti submarine nets. There we waited. As with the Sicilian invasion, we heard on the radio news that there had been another landing—this time on the western Italian mainland at a place called Salerno, just south of Naples. This was to be our next destination.

Rumours were that things were not going too well. We left in convoy in daylight and passed through the Straits of Messina. In the evening light we saw to port on an opposite course the well-known old battleship HMS Warspite. Down at the head and with a destroyer escort, she looked a bit sad. She had been one of the bombarding squadron at the landing and we heard later that she had been hit (twice I think) by Jerry's latest secret weapon—radio controlled glider bombs.

The German planes made a determined effort to disrupt and destroy our shipping but were not really successful. Then in the gathering darkness, again off to port, the volcanic island of Stromboli was seen erupting, giving us a really attractive spectacle, with red-hot ash shooting skywards and lava running down the slopes. It looked for all the world like the fireworks we used to have on November the fifth.

We came up to the Salerno anchorage the next day: it seemed peaceful enough. We were urged to anchor as close inshore as possible. There seemed to be a gently shelving beach and no one else was very close in. The Old Man was wary and we got out the old hand lead line to take soundings as we approached, anchoring in the front rank. Then we had time to look around and take stock.

Gunfire could be heard and we saw that a wrecked landing craft on the shoreline was being shelled. We had a little chuckle that Jerry was wasting his shells. Just to port of us our neighbour had already starting discharging its motor transport on to a large flat motorised barge that was moored alongside. Suddenly there was a loud bang, smoke and a shower of sparks—a shell had landed on the edge of the barge. Our Old Man didn't wait to find out more, it was "Heave up the anchor, we're shifting!" but it was only to a less exposed position. No doubt some of the ships' crews already there had a quiet chuckle at our discomfiture.

The anchorage was surrounded and overlooked by hills, in which there were railway tunnels, but this area had not yet been captured and cleared by our forces. We were told that Jerry had guns mounted on rail wagons that he trundled out on the track in order to let off a few rounds, before ducking back into the tunnels again.

The Royal Engineers' docks operating companies and the Pioneers again carried out the discharging. They stayed on board, dossing down where they could and having their meals brought out to them. There was an officer with them who stayed on board, sleeping on a saloon settee. One night he, the Second Mate and myself were sitting in my cabin, when at about ten o'clock he said he'd better do the rounds before turning in and off he went. It was pitch dark and he'd not been gone long when there were sounds of a scuffle outside and cries of "Help! Help!" The Second Mate and I dashed out with torches and immediately there was the clatter of hobnailed boots on the steel deck as two or three people ran off. We found the officer lying crumpled in the alleyway outside my cabin. He said his assailants had been trying to push him overboard! He was unharmed but badly shaken.

In our deep tanks we were carrying NAAFI stores which included cigarettes and spirits. It had been arranged for lorries to be 'parked' on the lids of the deep tanks to keep their contents secure, but somehow or other a way in had been found. The officer on his rounds had become suspicious that something untoward was going on and an attempt had been made to silence him. Next morning signals were made to shore. A small army vessel arrived alongside and three squaddies were taken ashore under the escort of MPs.

We had the occasional air raid warning, but nothing serious developed so our lads must have secured air supremacy. Despite the fracas with the army lieutenant, the discharging went on very efficiently since much had been learned from the experience in Sicily. Particularly useful were the large flat barges already mentioned and more landing craft had been obtained to replace the vulnerable DUKWs.

Empty once more, we went back to Augusta and then on to Tripoli for another load, this time destined for Bari on the Adriatic coast. We sailed around the instep of Italy until we got to Taranto and there we stayed for a day or two, anchored in the outer harbour. It was hot. Everyone longed for a swim but we were surrounded by jellyfish, hundreds of them of all sizes—and jellyfish sting—or we thought they did. One brave fellow went down a rope ladder, examined one, turned it over with a piece of wood, carefully touched it once, twice—nothing happened! Soon there were two opposing forces in the water, slinging jellyfish at each other. No one came to any harm, but there was a high mortality rate for the jellyfish of Taranto.

Bari, which had been captured by the Allies on September the 22nd 1943, was in those days a pleasant little harbour town on the eastern or Adriatic side of Italy. Owing to the Allies wish to keep it as a headquarters base, it had been little damaged. I believe we actually made two trips there. It was my job as the junior officer to supervise the unloading at night-time and such was the urgency to get the supplies ashore we worked shifts under full deck lights. None of us was very happy about this, but we were told that Jerry was not in a position to mount bombing raids and that seemed to be the case.

Again we carried NAAFI stores and again some enterprising squaddies found a way in. At six a.m. one morning at the end of my shift I went on the rounds preparatory to handing over to the Second Mate. As I walked around number two hold 'tween decks I could hear moaning from behind some crates and when I shone my torch, there was a squaddie as drunk as a coot, unable to get up or talk coherently. I went up the ladder to look over the side and could see the squaddies formed up there, ready to march off, so I called out to the NCO in charge, "Hey, you've left one aboard!"

Consternation! There was some consultation down there before two MPs came aboard and went down into the hold. What they did I don't know, but in the space of a few minutes they not only had the chappie walking, but he climbed up the vertical ladder out of the hatchway. They took him ashore and inserted him into the lines with the other men but no sooner had the MPs walked away than he tried to abscond! Eventually order was restored and they all marched off. A few days later an army car came to collect me to give evidence at his court martial. I was given lunch at the army officers' mess, which to everyone's amusement was situated on the opposite side of the road to and overlooking the local brothel.

I can't account for all our ship's movements in the Med. at this time, as we were not supposed to keep diaries, although I think it's pretty obvious that some people did do so. A considerable amount of time was spent waiting for convoys to get under way and although the distances travelled from one place to another were not great, progress was rather slow. We had to follow the routes swept free by minesweepers.

Mail was irregular, but marvellously, it did arrive. Sending it, however, was not all that easy. We couldn't write when or as often as we wished and it had to go through the official channels via the Censor. Sometimes we could buy Airmail Letters, which were the best and maybe the civilian version is still around. They comprised a single sheet of light blue paper, rather smaller than A4 in size and one could write all over one side and half of the back, then fold it into four and send it off. A second less satisfactory type was the Air Letter Card, which again was a single sheet rather less than A4 in size, but one could write only on one side and not too small. This was because they were photographed, reduced in size to about a quarter and then delivered like that. Thirdly, and least satisfactory of all (I can't even remember its name) was a sheet containing a numbered list of ready-made phrases, such as, "All my love", "I am well" and so on. One could choose four of these by writing down the numbers. It made for a rather stilted 'letter', but it did have the advantage that it didn't require literary inspiration.

On December 2nd 1943, precisely two weeks after we had left, the small port of Bari suffered what has been described as the worst shipping disaster since Pearl Harbour. The Germans had decided that something must be done to halt the influx of material to the Eighth Army and they mounted a 'once and for all raid'. Their reconnaissance planes had spotted a harbour full of shipping with a newly arrived convoy waiting to enter. Junkers 88s flew low down the Adriatic from a northern airfield, met up with a contingent from Yugoslavia and under cover of darkness came in low over the sea. For some reason the shore radar was not working that night and surprise was complete.

Cargo was being worked and lights were full on, the ships loaded with bombs and ammunition and a tanker moored at the oil jetty. Under ordinary circumstances, this would have been bad enough, but one of the American Liberty ships was secretly loaded with one hundred tons of mustard gas bombs and they went up with everything else. The story is too long to be told here but seventeen ships were lost, including the Polish Lwow which had taken me home from Gibraltar, six were damaged but survived and over a thousand Allied personnel and Italian civilians lost their lives. The whole thing was hushed up (because of the presence of the mustard gas as much as anything else, even though it was only being held for retaliation) but we did hear rumours. I was not aware of the scale of the tragedy until fifty eight years later when one day, walking through Tower Street in Ludlow, I saw in a charity shop a paper back book entitled 'Disaster at Bari' (Disaster at Bari by Glenn Infield, New English Library, 1976). Yet again I had been lucky.

Passing the port of Bougie in darkness (these ports all have different names now) on the way to Algiers, there was an air raid in progress. From afar, as with the eruption at Stromboli, such events can look quite pretty, with arcs of tracer fire converging on the target like an open umbrella punctuated with white stars from the heavier ack ack bursts. Our young Arab firemen had probably not seen such a thing before and they came up on deck to have a look.

A couple of planes flew fairly low over the convoy and we opened up on them. What goes up has to come down and a few Oerlikon 20mm. shells landed on our steel after deck, exploding on impact and scattering small pieces of hot shell casing, some of which penetrated the soft fleshy calves and posteriors of our firemen. There was much wailing, not so much from the sufferers but from their friends who were wailing on their behalf. The Spanish steward had handed over the 'medical duties' to the Second Mate. He had the 'wounded' laid face down on the pantry floor, with a couple of their friends to hold them down and do the moaning, praying or whatever. With my assistance, using peroxide, cotton wool, scalpel and tweezers, we removed the offending jagged pieces of metal. No real harm was done, but it would be something to boast about when they got home.

I can't remember where we spent Christmas 1943 but I feel sure we were in Algiers for New Year. I can remember going up to the bridge at midnight: all the ships were blowing their steam whistles and I rang sixteen bells—eight for the old year going out and eight for the new year coming in—all of us feeling a bit homesick.

We must have left in a UK bound convoy soon after and as the Gibraltar Straits fell well astern a FW Condor latched on and flew around us. We were quite used to that by then, but this one decided to have a go at us and came in from astern of the convoy. He was no hero of the master race and was far too high to attack with any accuracy. Up on Monkey Island, I saw the bombs leave the plane and give a flash in the sunlight as they fell seawards—then it was just a case of waiting. The plane was far too high and out of range of any of our anti aircraft fire. I felt sure that the bombs would 'land' on the far side of the convoy but it was quite a relief when they did, splashing harmlessly between two columns of ships. That was the last 'action' of the voyage.

We paid off in Barry, South Wales, on 20th January 1944, the end of a voyage for which we had been signed on under some kind of wartime Sea Transport Articles. I had been very surprised during the voyage, when the Mate told me that hours worked over eight (or perhaps nine or ten, I can't remember) in one day counted as overtime and one could take the money or leave in lieu. I should therefore keep a check on them. Owing to my twelve-hour night shifts at various times, I had accrued quite a bit and on paying off I opted to take it as leave. We had been away for something over seven months, which qualified for eighteen days leave, but I also got another ten days bonus! Obviously, the ship was not going to wait around without a Third Mate for twenty-eight days and the only way to take the leave was to pay off, which I did.

I've said before that there was little to do in wartime Darlaston, but that mattered little—Edna and I had each other.

There was a strange sequel to the Fort Walsh voyage. The Second Mate, whose name was Jones, came from the small town of Llanrwst in North Wales. He was a few years older than I was but we soon became friends. He had a girl friend, a sergeant in the ATS, who was of some concern to him in that he was uncertain whether she was being loyal to him. Some two or three months into the voyage he stopped speaking to me socially and withdrew into himself, saying only what was necessary in the course of our duties. It didn't matter a great deal to me, as I had other friends and if that was the way he wanted it, so be it. When we arrived at aforementioned Algiers and received some mail, he started speaking to me again as though nothing had been amiss. I concluded, rightly or wrongly, that it had something to do with his love affair. When we signed off I thought no more about it, but imagine my amazement when, after I had been home on leave for about two weeks, a telegram came asking me to be best man at his wedding! The whole idea seemed so time consuming and impracticable that I had to wire back to wish them well and say it was not possible.

I see from my discharge book that my time on board the Fort Walsh was seven months and twenty days. I have discovered that in 1948 she was sold to the Italians, then in 1965 she passed to a Haitian firm and was renamed the Ti Hi. She was broken up in 1967.

16

OPERATION DRAGOON—THE SOUTH OF FRANCE INVASION

The Ocean Gypsy—who said tipsy?

Why my recall came from Liverpool when I had signed off previously in Barry I don't know, but that is what happened. When I got to the Pool office I was asked to join the Ocean Gypsy lying in Salford docks, Manchester. So it was back to Lime Street station, buy a ticket, get kit out of left luggage office and find a train to Manchester. I'm not sure how one got from Manchester to Salford in those days—it would either be by tram or local train. In many cities servicemen could go anywhere on the tramcar for one penny and we in the Merchant Service were allowed that facility too.

I got to the docks in the afternoon to find no ship—I was told she had gone down the canal to Birkenhead! I found a meal and then reversed the journey back again. When I finally got to the Birkenhead dock gates it was dark. I asked the gate policeman where the Ocean Gypsy was lying: he checked his list but she wasn't there! He telephoned a few numbers and the consensus of opinion was that she had missed the tide and must be anchored out in the Mersey. She should come into dock about eight o'clock the next morning.

There seemed no point in trying to get a boat to ferry me out there so I asked the policeman if he could recommend somewhere to stay for the night, thinking he might know of some small local hotel. Instead, and I was in 'civvies' at the time, he pointed over to the other side of the road and said, "There's the Sally Army over there, you'll get a good bed and breakfast for half a crown." Well, that was something I hadn't done before, but if it was any good it would save a lot of trouble, so I went to have a look. There was just one large dormitory with about thirty beds, all spotlessly neat, clean and as far as I could see only one other inhabitant. I booked in, stowed my kit around one of the beds and went for a cup of tea and something to eat. I remember that when I turned in I slept on my wallet, but I need not have done. I slept well and had an excellent breakfast too next morning. By the time I got back to the dock gates the Ocean Gypsy was alongside the quay. They were as glad to see me as I was to see them.

As I've said before, the 'Ocean' boats were the American built versions of the standard design merchant ships, similar to the Empires and Forts, so everything was immediately familiar. Being American built though, there was much more welding used in their construction. The Gypsy had good quality accommodation and a few extra trimmings as well, such as the two ten-inch searchlights on the monkey island fitted with shutters for daylight signalling.

J & C Harrison of London, a well-known firm, managed the ship. She had made her maiden voyage from the USA to northern Russia in December 1943, as a participant in the convoy that the battle-cruiser Scharnhorst had attempted to attack. The outcome, however, had been the sinking of the Scharnhorst by the Royal Navy. The crewmembers remaining on board were still excited by these events and would relate them to anyone who was prepared to listen.

It was February 22nd 1944 when I signed on. The Captain was a large pear shaped man in his fifties named Nesbit, who we were to find had a great liking for brandy. The First Mate was Alec Pain: in his thirties, smallish, fair-haired, quiet but very competent, he lived in Liverpool. During the Nineteen Thirties slump, after he had finished his apprenticeship and was unable to get a ship, he had worked as an attendant at Wolverhampton Corporation Baths, so we had something in common. Alec took his responsibilities very seriously and it was apparent to me that he had become a Harrison Company man and was hoping for an eventual command. We got on well together. The Second Mate was an odd bod: a short dark Welshman with features rather like Mr. Punch, he must have been the same age as the Old Man. We found he had a similar liking for the brandy, which may have been his undoing in his younger days and could have explained why he was still only Second Mate. Nevertheless, we got on well together.

The Old Man seemed to take to me at once and it was not long before he was sending me over to the offices in Liverpool to do the ship's business for him, "to save him the bother". It was not much bother. I used to order a taxi to take me there and back through the Mersey Tunnel, with the recommendation to try a pub by the agent's office where the "oysters, pork pie and Guinness are very good", all on expenses.

We began loading much the same military cargo as on my previous ships, so we were obviously going back to somewhere in the Med. This was confirmed, when just before we sailed a small group of army officers arrived. They were AMGOT (Allied Military Government of Occupied Territories) personnel, in civilian life police officers, customs officials, local government officers etc. and it would be their job to impose allied government on occupied towns, using existing officials where appropriate. They were going to Italy and used the voyage to bring their planning up to date. I remember being very impressed by the intelligence they had, with comprehensive printed books listing the towns of Italy, naming the Mayors and many of the towns' officials.

They were a merry lot. We had no passenger accommodation so they had to fit in where they could with some of them sleeping in the saloon and one of them dossing down on my cabin settee. One of them in civilian life was a police inspector from Bromley and he had a photographic memory. His party trick was for someone to give him an unfamiliar book and point out a paragraph, which he would then read aloud and immediately recite word for word without further reference.

By now the defeated U-boats had been withdrawn from the Atlantic and our passage to the Meddy in March 1944 was pretty well routine. We went to Naples, since I suppose Bari had become unusable, but Naples was also showing signs of damage. Edna's younger brother Stan, who was in the army, was supposed to be there somewhere but although I spent a day ashore trying to find him I got nowhere. Some of us went to an ENSA show at the Opera House. I remember being greatly impressed by the talent of one young female singer of popular ballads who had a whole house of raucous squaddies quite tamed and hanging on every word. Occasionally we had a few vinos at the Officers' Club and that was about it. The Old Man's taste for cognac was becoming apparent, likewise the Chief Engineer. The Ocean Gypsy was becoming known to some of us as the Ocean Tipsy.

From Naples, it was south again to Tripoli, where we were to embark a company of the REME (Royal Electrical and Mechanical Engineers) and take them over to Italy. These skilled craftsmen, of many and varied trades, had advanced through the Libyan Desert with the Eighth Army. All their workshop equipment, stores, transport and so on had to be loaded aboard, the most cosseted item of which was a silver Mercedes saloon which had been 'liberated' by their South African Brigadier. He actually came to see it craned aboard. It was probably their carpenters who erected in our 'tween decks some hundred or so three tier bunks for the other ranks, with the officers sleeping in our accommodation as before. They brought their own field kitchen and cooks and fed themselves. The OC troops believed in keeping his men busy and pestered Alec into finding work for his men to do. They were a grand lot and it was a pleasure to have them aboard.

By the time we delivered the REME ashore in Italy it was late May 1944. We then sailed to Algiers, together with a number of other ships, and there we tied up stern-on to the mole with an anchor out forward. We wondered why this was—we had thought we might be on our way home.

I taught the three sparkies who had nothing to do how to 'drive' the motored lifeboat and go alongside in the approved manner.

They were then able to go along to the naval post office each day and collect any mail. We also ran a 'liberty boat' ashore in the evening but Alec insisted that I had to be there on the return run to 'maintain discipline' as some of the leave men were likely to be the worse for wear.

The young Third Mate and a couple of the apprentices on our neighbouring ship had bought an Enterprise dinghy from somewhere for twelve pounds and they made me welcome aboard. We used to go out for an evening sail just before sunset, always giving the sentry at the harbour entrance a hail as we went out so that he would know when we came back that we were not saboteurs.

Although I can not now remember the details we then made a couple of trips ferrying stores and equipment to the newly restored port of Bari. Following this, there was considerable dismay when, instead of being sent back to the UK, we were sent eastwards along the coast to Bizerta where we anchored in the lake in company with many other ships, and there we stuck. I think we stayed there for four or five weeks of absolute boredom. The lake at Bizerta is not a very scenic place, it tends to get very still and hot. I built myself a four poster bed complete with tester on the after end of the bridge deck and slept up there in the cool.

If someone had said to us, "Since you have the right types of ships and the experience, we are keeping you here preparatory to the invasion of Southern France", we would have been more content, but of course for security reasons nobody could tell us that, so we just fretted. This invasion was an event which had been conceived to take place at the same time as, or even before, the Normandy landings but planning disputes and procrastination so continued to delay the launch date that one could argue its time of usefulness had passed. The Normandy invasion duly took place in June and we felt left right out of things. Even more ships arrived, which seemed such a waste and as always it's not knowing what is going on that is the worst part.

Edna and I had a tacit agreement that we would wed after I had obtained my First Mates 'ticket'. It was by then becoming apparent that I would have enough sea-time to do that the next time we got home. Since I could get twelve weeks study leave it seemed daft to wait until after the exams—why not get married first and have an extended honeymoon? I put the proposal in a letter to my intended and she approved, saw the vicar and 'had the banns called' in anticipation. I started to catch up on some serious studying.

Occasionally I and a couple of the sparkies would take the Old Man in to Bizerta on some business or other, or maybe he needed to stock up on cognac—actually these were quite sober days—and with luck he would bring back some mail. By this time our shorts, shirts, underwear and socks were beginning to wear out and it seemed impossible to interest anyone in our problem. The difficulty was solved by our chief gunner, a long service Sergeant of Marines, who found a mildly corrupt army quartermaster who for a few pound notes and a great deal of secrecy supplied enough gear to 'keep shirts on our backs'. From then on I was an enthusiastic wearer of army socks.

It might be appropriate here to mention the Mission to Seamen's Library Service, which as far as I know was run entirely by volunteers. Before we sailed, someone would deliver a 'library' of two wooden boxes containing about sixty books of all kinds, fiction and non-fiction, and recover the previous issue. Keeping track of them and who had borrowed what was another chore passed on to the Third Mate. Usually there was not time for a lot of reading but at places like Bizerta these books were a godsend. I remember I found the paper-backed edition of H G Wells' History of the World. From that book I saw the breadth and scope of history as I had never seen it before. Spurned by academics he might have been, but he struck sparks of illumination where they failed.

At last we moved, to Tunis. Here we changed our allegiance: we were no longer with the Eighth Army, now we would transport the Yanks. By this time, as well as our clothes wearing thin, so was our larder and our rations had to be supplemented from their army stores. Much of it was well liked by me (dare I mention Spam?) The tinned bacon, rolled with paper between each slice to aid its unpacking, was superb.

Our cargo was much the same as before: military stores, ammo, jeeps, a large number of trucks. I don't remember loading tanks;

perhaps they all went on the specialist tank landing ships. The American troops, just over 300 of them, slept in the 'tween deck bunks previously put in by the REME and their officers billeted in our accommodation. One of their field kitchens was put on number-two hatch, in front of and just below the bridge. On sea watch at elevenses I was handed up treacle flapjacks and coffee! We were of course taking them to the South of France invasion, Operation Dragoon, which commenced on August 15th 1944 although I think we arrived on the following day.

I have very clear memories of the operation, with the clean sandy beach and high sand cliffs behind. There were not many of us there, just five or six ships anchored off shore, unloading into the landing craft. I've always had it in my mind that our landing was close to St. Tropez, although there was no habitation in sight. When Edna and I went to the coast of the South of France many years later and visited the monument to the landings I was puzzled. Its position did not match with my memory of the landing at all. However, I now know that there were landings at more than one location and my memory is in fact correct. We took our Americans to the Pampelonne beach, which runs north-south just a few kilometres south of St. Tropez, whereas the monument is at Cape du Dramont which is much nearer to Cannes. Although there had initially been some very fierce fighting in certain locations, our area was quiet except for the odd visit by a Jerry recce' plane. The operation was, as we said then, 'a piece of cake'. (I read recently that by August 31st, 184,000 troops were put ashore with 191,230 tons of supplies and 39,390 vehicles. Putting that another way, there was one vehicle for every 4.6 men).

We were sent back to North Africa for another load. A letter from Edna arrived saying the banns had expired and she was having them called again. By the time we were loaded Marseilles had been 'liberated' and to there we were bound, only carrying cargo this time—no troops, no treacle flapjacks.

A few days out in the early afternoon, the alarm went. I ran up to the monkey island. There was a bit of low mist and flying to our left, low down on the port side of the convoy and just out of range, was a long line of twelve or thirteen Junkers 88 torpedo bombers. They crossed astern of us, flew up the starboard side of the convoy and turned in, in line abreast. We were left of centre in the convoy. Most of the ships on the starboard side were US liberty ships and the Americans believed in fire power—remember I said they had an anti-aircraft gun on the foc'stle as well as all their other armaments. The field of fire they put up was simply terrific, in fact I thought it was frightening that the inner ships opened up as well, they must surely have sprayed their fellow ships. It must have frightened Jerry too because they all broke off their run-in and turned away out of range. Probably stern words were spoken and they formed up for another try, to be met with at least the same welcome as before, but they were more determined the second time. Three planes carried on right over the convoy. What was incredible was that not a plane came down and not a ship was torpedoed! These were not the Jerry pilots of old!

Then came an incident, the whereabouts of which I have not been able to locate. During the evening on the Mate's watch, as we neared the French coast, a few ships including ours were told to anchor between two islands. I went up to the bridge to relieve Alec, so that he could go on the foc'stle head to superintend the anchoring. I could see the Old Man was well fortified but he seemed to be carrying it well. As we approached the anchorage he left the bridge and didn't return. What should I do? If I shouted through the megaphone to Alec the whole ship would know! I decided to carry on and anchor the ship myself—I had seen it done often enough. All went well, I did all the right things and Alec was impressed, although the Old Man never mentioned it afterwards.

As it happened we had a terrible night. A very fierce off shore wind sprang up—I guess it was a katabatic wind from the French Alps—and it blew gustily. We started to drag anchor. We had to veer and let go a second anchor, but still we dragged. The Old Man was back in circulation again and for a while we had to steam slow ahead on the anchors in order to maintain position. I have just not been able to decide where this excitement took place. The only islands I can find in the atlas near to Marseilles are those to the south of Cap Croisette and they seem too near the mainland, so perhaps they were those near Ile Ratonneau.

When daylight broke the wind dropped and that afternoon we steamed in to Marseilles. The port area looked very bomb damaged and derelict as we entered and we berthed a very long way from the Old Port. In the evening some of us made a determined effort to see some of the sights, but there was no transport running so we walked—for about three-quarters of an hour—until we found a small cafe. We had a couple of glasses of wine and walked back—so much for the 'Cesspool of Europe'.

Somewhere in amongst all this toing, froing and blowing passed Christmas 1944 and the New Year 1945, but where we were then I don't know. Then came the best news of the voyage—we were to go to Valencia to load oranges! That could only mean one thing—we were going home with the first 'commercial' cargo since I had left the Saint Merriel.

It was grand to be in a place for a while that had no blackout. I was able to go ashore for an afternoon and buy a wristwatch for Edna. The Old Man, the Chief and the Second Mate gave themselves up to the delights of Spanish cognac. The Old Man had obtained two large glass pickle jars from the steward, into which he'd put quantities of cherries and topped them up with cheap Spanish cognac—he said it 'took the fire out'—and called it cherry brandy. Alec was concerned that the crates of oranges should be stowed properly with built in ventilation tunnels and that no hidden time bombs were in amongst them. Although Spain was neutral, there was always the danger of sabotage by enemy agents. The dockers knew their job and didn't have to be told what to do, but as for any bombs all we could do was to look vigilant and there were only two of us.

We loaded only a part cargo at Valencia before going about sixty miles up the coast to the small port of Burriana to top up. The Second Mate was still 'hors de combat' so I went up to the chartroom to lay off the courses. The Old Man was by now on his feet, the pilot came aboard and we cast off. Even before we got as far as the pilot boat the Old Man had disappeared. I dropped the pilot, streamed the log and rang 'Full Speed Ahead'. Having stowed away his anchors and put things ship shape Alec came up to the bridge, saw how things were and asked, "You're all right here? I've got things to do. I'll relieve you for dinner. Cheerio". There I was—in command! (But only 'acting' as they say in the services). Nevertheless, it was a great experience.

I'd had another letter from Edna to say the banns had expired yet again and the vicar was pulling her leg about a reluctant bridegroom. In order to buy a double bed she had had to apply for dockets or coupons, and had asked the vicar to write a letter to say that she was getting married and it was a genuine application.

She must have been very relieved when she got my telegram from Liverpool to say we had arrived and she could fix the date for the wedding. She had had all the work and preparation to do. I merely went home and got married.

Subsequent History of the Ocean Gypsy.
The Ocean Gypsy was built in Portland, Main. My time on board was 1 year 1 month and 13 days. After I left on 4th March 1945 she still had just over twenty years of service to go.

In September 1945, still managed by J & C Harrison, she took part in the invasion of Malaya but hostilities had ceased and there was no opposition.

In 1948 she went to the Clan Line, a Clyde shipping company which owned well founded and distinguished ships which tramped all over the world. I seem to remember they were crewed by Lascars and usually carried four apprentices or cadets. She was renamed the Clan MacBride.

In 1956 the Clan Line merged with the Union Castle Shipping Co. and formed the British & Commonwealth Shipping Co.

1958 saw her sold to the Valles Steamship Co. of Panama—a sign of things to come perhaps?—and she was renamed the Alice.

In May 1966 she went aground at Kuantan off the east coast of Malaya, was refloated but broken up for scrap at Hirao in June.

17

SPLICING

Marriage, Honeymoon and First Mate's Ticket

A thirteen month long voyage, with leave accumulated at two and a half days per month, gave thirty two days shore leave and with study leave still to be added things were looking good.

The big thing that had to be arranged was the honeymoon, which was not easy in wartime Britain. I suggested that we stay with the Davids in Cardiff if they would take us. Edna agreed—it had happy memories—and Mabel wrote back to say yes, they would take us. The wedding service was held at St. George's Church, Darlaston at ten in the morning on Tuesday March 20th 1945. Edna was a regular member of that church in those days and some time previously I had been 'interviewed' by her vicar: I suppose he wanted to see if I was worthy of his young parishioner, but if he gave her his opinion she never told it to me.

It was a commendably short service, but I couldn't understand why there were so many people there, including most of the staff from Edna's office. A small number of guests joined us for a meal at my parents' house, Alvan, and then we left at twelve noon to catch the train to Cardiff. The Davids made us really welcome, with the old lady seeming particularly pleased to see us wed. The weather stayed fine for us. There was an effective public transport system in those days and we made excursions into the country and to the seaside. We had a quiet time to ourselves for about a week.

For some reason I had decided to attempt the First Mate's examinations in Liverpool—the college there had a good reputation—so having had a few days back at Darlaston we set out once again. At Liverpool we went to see the Billeting Officer who sent us to an address in Waterloo on the north side of the city. The accommodation offered was not up to Park Lane standards but it wasn't bad, with a large front sitting cum dining room downstairs, upstairs bed and bath, shared kitchen downstairs. Edna said it would suit. It was convenient for me, in that just a few yards away at the end of the street was the bus stop into the city and the college. There were local shops nearby and beyond them, not far away, was the Mersey shore.

I registered at the college. I would take the bus in the mornings and get back late in the afternoons, leaving Edna to sort out rationing and shopping in a strange locality. Not far away from the college was a department store that had a restaurant. Edna came in on the bus or tram one day and we went there for midday lunch. After a pleasant meal the waitress gave us our bill and left us. When I opened the bill it was just for two coffees. Was it a mistake? The waitress was no longer there to ask, so I paid the bill and left. It then became part of our routine to lunch there once a week. We made sure we always sat in that waitress's area and always the bill was for two coffees. I didn't wear uniform to go to college, but all of us wore the small 'MN' badge in our lapels and Edna had a small silver and enamel 'MN' brooch I had given her. Edna thought the waitress must have had a soft spot for the Merchant Navy and maybe had a boyfriend in the service.

When I was a small boy Father had taken me to see the Liverpool Maritime Museum that I found so fascinating. I decided I would take Edna there so that she could see what had influenced me in my younger days. We walked up the broad frontal steps to a glass-enclosed cubicle at the top. A uniformed attendant greeted us and I said I had brought my wife to show her the museum. 'Certainly Sir' he said and emerged from his cubicle to take us inside, as I thought, but when we passed through a screen there was nothing there, just a great hole. The building had been hit in the bombing and the street frontage was all that was left. Thank goodness the exhibits had been moved elsewhere beforehand. It was typical of much of Liverpool—indeed of all the large towns and cities—where there were large areas of dereliction and tidied up bomb damage.

After a while Edna began to suffer from morning sickness and she did suffer too. Rations were meagre and many items had to be queued for, which was an ordeal for her in that state. She told me one day that she had almost fainted and had been swiftly sent to the front of the queue by sympathetic housewives.

We were able to go to the occasional concert in the city and for one week there were performances by an operatic company. We went to see 'La Boheme'. The reigning diva at the time was an Australian soprano named Joan Hammond. A squarish well built woman, she was not well cast physically as the diminutive Mimi dying of consumption in a Parisian garret, but this was wartime. Anyway, she could certainly sing—no microphones were necessary.

It was still my intention to make a career at sea and I thought it was probably time to settle down and establish my future with some shipping firm, in other words to become a 'company's man'. I fancied tankers. These ships were strong and safe, since they were divided into many small watertight compartments. The living conditions were above average, they paid 7.5% above the rate and they did regular runs. Against this was the fact that they spent little time in port since liquids are quickly pumped, but wives were welcome on board. Their cargoes could be dangerous and volatile but there was in Liverpool the United Molasses Co., which owned tankers under the Athel Line name. These had regular trade with the Caribbean, bringing back molasses of course and that was safe enough. I talked it over with Edna and as a result I applied for a job with them. A few days later I was interviewed by their Marine Superintendent, who told me to get in touch with him when I had my 'ticket'.

The European war ended, to everyone's relief. For many it was a time of rejoicing and jubilation. I didn't feel that way. Certainly I was pleased it was over but I was too much concerned with thinking of all those we had lost to generate any gaiety and there were still the Japanese to overcome.

Examination week seemed to go all right. I thought the 'Oral Seamanship' examiner seemed satisfied, but all of us were worried about one of the questions in the 'Stability' paper which none of us could understand. However, enough marks must have been obtained and I passed—the date on my certificate is July 23rd 1945. I let the Athel Line know I had got my First Mate's Certificate. We packed and went back to Alvan.

My total time on shore had amounted to five months and four days.

18

END OF HOSTILITIES

The Atheltarn goes East.

Very soon I received a telegram asking me to join the SS Atheltarn in Falmouth as the Second Mate. With more concern than usual, for Edna was by then three months pregnant, I took a train that went direct via Bristol to Truro. I put all my kit into the Guard's van, with the exception of my sextant, which I took with me into the compartment. The train was packed but the crowd thinned out at Bristol. Arriving at Truro I was shocked and dismayed to find that my kit was not in the Guard's van. I reported to the stationmaster and was able to inform him that it was all correctly tagged and labelled. He said it had probably been wrongly taken out at Bristol—"Don't worry, it will turn up". I wasn't all that reassured. It meant that I had no toilet things, no pyjamas, and no change of clothes—nothing. However, I took the local train to Falmouth and found my ship.

A tarn is a small lake and the Atheltarn was a small ship—smaller than anything I had been on before. I reported to the Captain, told him my predicament and said that I was sorry but I obviously couldn't sign on without any kit. He was not very pleased but had to agree. I reckon he must have gone off and lit a few fires somewhere, as he obviously couldn't sail without his Second Mate. On the third day after my arrival a message came from Falmouth railway station to say that my kit was there. It was indeed and nothing had gone missing.

The ship was quite old and she was a coal burner! Could anything be more absurd than a coal burning oil tanker? She was only about half the length of my previous ships and had probably been built for a coastal trade. She had a raised foc'stle and poop, with an expansion trunk running lengthways between them which was straddled by the bridge and the accommodation block. Connecting all three 'houses' was a raised walkway or flying bridge that was positioned above the expansion trunk. Being a tanker, the engine room was located aft to keep any funnel sparks away from the inflammable cargo. The engineers lived aft as well but for meals they came along to the 'midships' saloon. We had only one Sparks, there being no accommodation for any others, but perhaps by this stage of the war it was thought that more were unnecessary.

The Third Mate was a twenty-one-year-old from Essex called Phillip Freshwater. He had served his time with the Athel Line, had just got his ticket and was making his first trip at that rank. We soon became good friends. The Mate, a Scot named Ferguson, was a little over forty and 'sweating' to get his first command. He was a decent fellow. A God fearing teetotaller who didn't swear, he quickly came to regard us as 'his boys'. We worked well with him and we made a good trio. The Old Man was about fifty, a smallish corpulent figure who was always concerned about his appearance and dignity. Surnamed White, he was immediately christened by the Third Mate as 'El Blanco' which was so apt it stuck. I think he was rather concerned about the youthful behaviour of his junior officers, but we were experienced and conscientious and didn't let him down.

We took on an Indian crew: Hindus on deck who lived forrard in the foc'stle, Muslims in the engine room who lived aft in the poop and Goan Christian cooks and stewards to look after 'the white men'. The exception was the Chief Steward who was white, a companies man we knew as Charlie. The Hindus and Muslims each had their own cooks and cooking arrangements.

It was no secret that we were 'going out East' but to do what? The most likely task was as a 'fleet oiler', topping up naval ships in some God forsaken hole in the Pacific. Two technicians came aboard and fitted up a Radio Telephone set on the bridge. Three small coastal-river boats were on their way out to Hong Kong and we were to 'mother' them as far as Gib in a sort of loose convoy.

On August 5th 1945 the first atom bomb was dropped on Japan. On August 8th the Articles of Agreement were signed (This was the contract of employment between captain and crew) and the next day the second bomb was dropped, which surely meant that the end was nigh! On the 15th August 1945 Japan surrendered—a tremendous relief. The next day was VJ Day and Falmouth erupted into celebrations. There was dancing in the streets. I wondered if those making the most noise had made the least contribution. I didn't feel like joining in the merriment and in the evening I walked through the town to the headland overlooking The Roads and thought of the past, the present and the future with Edna.

Maybe we wouldn't sail? We did, on the eighteenth, with no oil cargo loaded in the tanks. The Old Man and I went up to the chartroom and laid off the courses which it had been agreed would take us to Gib. Around the coast we had to keep to prescribed routes through the uncleared minefields but beyond them the seas were ours.

As soon as we got out into open water we ran into one of those fierce South Westerlies common to the Bay of Biscay and our 'convoy' ceased to exist; it was every man for himself. It was as much as we could do to look after ourselves, never mind anyone else. Although small and old the Atheltarn was a good seaboat, there were never any worries on that score, but what she could not do was make much headway against a head sea and our speed dropped considerably. One of our 'ducklings' got to Gib before we did!

As Second Mate I was responsible for the navigation. The Old Man also took part in the 'noon sights' ritual, as did the Third Mate. The Old Man used the same 'longitude by chronometer' method as Captain Owens had done, as did all the men of his generation, and I think he regarded with suspicion the new-fangled 'intercept method' which I used. However, he did get used to it and I wasn't going to change. I was also on the 'twelve to four', the middle or 'graveyard' watch. With no blackout, no convoy, no station keeping to worry about and everyone using navigation lights again, it was just like it had been when I joined over six years earlier. The stress had gone. When I got used to the short stretches of sleep either side of the graveyard, and I did manage it, I quite liked the arrangement. Nobody else was around after midnight except the other watch-keepers—the ship was mine! After midday, the Old Man and the Mate usually had an afternoon nap and so the ship was mine then too.

Having called at Gib we went on to Port Said, making what were to be the best days' runs of the voyage at an average of nine knots, thanks to a clean bottom and good coal, but never to be repeated. At Port Said we had to bunker. Two long planks were laid from the shore to the bunker hatch in front of the funnel. A long continuous line of 'coolies', each with a bag of coal on his shoulders, trotted up the rhythmically bouncing plank and each tipped his bag into the hatch, then trotted down the other plank for another one. Talk about labour intensive, but at least they had a job. This went on for hours.

From there we passed through the Suez Canal, new territory for me then, and down the stinking hot Red Sea to Aden. The southern part of the Red Sea from Jeddah onwards was quite interesting scenically and I enjoyed taking bearings of the peaks of that rather barren landscape to mark our position. Some of these had rather quaint names—I remember one double peak was called 'Asses Ears'. Having passed through the Straits of Bab el Mandeb we turned left for Aden. All I can say about Aden is that it's the sort of place one wants to leave quickly. Despite this, one good result of all the frequent stops was that we kept replenishing with fresh food and water.

Every time the Old Man went ashore we expected him to come back and say that it was all a mistake and that we were to turn round and take a cargo home. Not so, it was on to Bombay, which we reached on September 20th. We anchored in the river more or less opposite to the so-called Gateway of India and there we stuck for nearly four weeks. The Mate, who was more interested in cultural things than his two young proteges, organised for himself a boat trip to a local island where there were ancient Indian architectural remains. We thought this was a little eccentric but I've wished ever since that I had gone with him.

I didn't like Bombay, but I don't like cities anyway. I didn't like the congestion of both humans and traffic, the poverty of some of its citizens and in particular I didn't like the red spotted pavements, whereupon large quantities of betel juice had been spat.

It became clear that we hadn't been forgotten when we changed our Indian crew for another and sailed on to Colombo in Ceylon, now Sri Lanka. There we took up a more permanent attitude and moored stern on to a jetty with anchors down forrard. Our situation became very permanent and if the Old Man had any idea of what was going on he said nothing. It's difficult now to remember how we filled the time.

In the chartroom we had a large stock of Admiralty Charts and Sailing Directions for destinations all over the world. The latter were very interesting—some of the texts and drawn illustrations must have dated back to the sailing ship days of the nineteenth century, giving details of advised harbour approaches, landmarks, currents and soundings etc. Every so often the Admiralty issued Notices to Mariners, which gave details of any changes which had occurred since, perhaps necessitating a correction to a chart or an alteration to a Sailing Direction. Every so often a 'Notice' would come in over the radio which Sparky would write out and hand in to the chart room. It was the Second Mate's job to make the corrections and by the time we left Colombo I reckon we must have had the most immaculately corrected set of Charts and Directions ever.

We had with us a small motor boat, which was powered by a beautiful old-fashioned, single cylinder, four-stroke engine with lovely grey shiny enamel paint, shiny brass parts and a large heavy flywheel. It had to be started up on petrol and when warm switched over to paraffin, although it would have run on almost any fuel, I think. It needed an energetic turn of the flywheel to get it going but once started it was a great little chugger and enabled us to get about a bit. Again, Fergie was more interested in the sights than the rest of us were—we just wanted to get away—and the highlight of his trips ashore was to have afternoon tea at the Galle Face Hotel on the water front, 'Pukka Sahib' style.

We ate well. There is a suspicion that catering staff are always on the fiddle to make a bit on the side and I reckon that Charlie our chief steward was sharp enough to be there if anything was going. As far as I was concerned he was welcome to anything he made; the food was superb. There was a cooked breakfast preceded by grapefruit and/or cereals, a cooked light lunch at midday, afternoon tea at three thirty and a six or seven course dinner at seven in the evening. With no watch keeping to worry about, the Old Man and all his officers sat down together in the saloon. El Blanco, at the head of table, had a bit of a dampening effect on natural conviviality but the Chief was a great raconteur of hoary stories and was very fond of quoting bits of Shakespeare. Other gastronomic delights were at the important religious celebrations of the Hindu and Muslim sections of our crew, when they cooked and served special meals for us.

Christmas and New Year were spent in Colombo but I have no memories of them. I decided I had better take some momentos home so I went ashore to look around the curio shops. They turned out to be mostly carved elephants of course. I spotted the one we now have as a table lamp and was questioning the shop proprietor about the type of wood and so on, when he asked me if I would like to see his 'elephant factory'. I said I certainly would and he took me through the rear door into the back yard. It was about the size of a normal domestic dining room and sitting around cross legged with their backs to the walls were his operatives, about a dozen of them, using saws, files and rasps. As he said, his products were definitely hand made.

Later in January 1946 there was a sign of movement and we paid off the Indian crew and took on Chinese. The Indians had done well, since they had received three months pay for working on board and had hardly been to sea. (Talking of pay, when the war ended and the end of our war bonus was nigh, the unions negotiated for it to become part of our wages so nothing changed really). We had instructions to go back to Bombay! This was all very puzzling but it was more or less in the direction we wanted to go. The chances of being sent further East to act as an oiler for the Royal Navy now seemed to have disappeared. Clearly the slow grind of bureaucracy was only now catching up with real events.

The Chinese crew, as enterprising business men, had made a purchase of fish which they gutted, filleted and hung up to dry in the sun on the foc'stle head. Like the Indians, they had their own galley and cooks. On the day we sailed, as we turned out of the harbour into a head wind, amidships on the bridge and in our accommodation we were immediately assaulted by an overwhelming smell of over ripe fish. There was a peremptory blast on Fergie's whistle and terse instructions were given to "Get that stuff moved aft".

It was during our second call at Bombay that I received a telegram to say that mother and boy were fine. I was a father; I had a son with all that it implied! I began to have second thoughts about whether to continue with a career at sea. It didn't seem right that Edna should have all the work and responsibility of bringing up our child (or children?). Not only did I think I ought to take my share, I very much wanted to play my part. Demobilisation of the armed forces had begun on a points system that took into account length of service, family responsibilities and so on. To avoid the calamity of all merchant ships losing their crews overnight, a similar system was in force for us. Thousands and thousands of young men (and women) were in a situation wherein they had joined up straight from school, university or employment and would now have to make a new civilian career for themselves.

If I was going to make a change it would make sense to do it sooner rather than later. Furthermore, because of my length of service and my new family responsibilities, I would have a low release number and be early in the queue, an advantage when looking for opportunities. I wrote to Edna to ask her opinion. The reply when it came was not helpful. It was to the effect that when she married me she married a sailor and had gone into it with her eyes open. She had considered what was involved and was prepared to accept the responsibilities. If I wanted to make a change it was up to me; she would back me up in what I decided but it would have to be my decision.

In the meantime I went ashore and bought some yards of Indian cotton print. I had no idea what for, but later it made some useful and attractive house jackets for the young mother.

We were directed back to the UK from Bombay. Our return voyage was a reversal of the passage outward, except for one or two details. When we stopped at Aden we loaded a full cargo of fuel oil in just a few hours, which put us 'down to our marks' for the first time in the voyage. It gave us a 'freeboard' of only five inches—that was the height of the main deck above the water line! Lying at anchor with a little lop on the water the waves washed inboard! It was not as bad as it sounds though, as the expansion trunk gave us about another three and a half feet and the flying bridge about another one and a half above that. At sea, most of the ship was underwater with just the three islands on show. With by then a weedy bottom and poor coal, we struggled to make eight knots at times, although in the smoother Red Sea with a following wind we averaged nine.

At Port Said we bunkered again and set out for Gibraltar. Westerly gales were blowing and it was rough. In the short seas of the Meddy we were buffeted badly, riding the swells like a horse over the jumps. Every so often the pitching would get out of sequence with the swells and the foc'stle head would be buried as tons of water came aboard. The engine had to be throttled down so that we were just making headway. There was no real danger, but people had to be careful not to lose their grip when moving along the flying bridge. In seven and a half days steaming at just over five knots we had only got as far as Malta so the Old Man decided to call in and bunker again. It was a welcome break, but things were not much better when we got out to sea again and it was another six days at just over seven knots before we made Gib.

I told Fergie I was thinking of 'swallowing the hook'. He said I couldn't do it—"Once the seawater gets in your veins Laddie, you've had it. Ye'll be back". He nevertheless gave me some good advice, which was "When you can afford it, invest in Scottish Widows". I didn't really know what he was talking about then, but I always remembered it, and later on acted on it.

Two events clinched my decision. We made a better passage across the Bay to the UK so perhaps the Chief had got his whip out. It was 'Falmouth for orders', just as in the sailing ship days and once there the orders were for Dublin. As we steamed up the Irish Sea my release number was heard on the radio news. That was the first event, which seemed a portent.

We arrived in Dublin next day and began cleaning the tanks as they were emptied. There seemed to be some haste to get things done and the ship back into commercial service again. After four days we were off, across to Birkenhead and we berthed there on March 19th 1946, the eve of our first wedding anniversary. I hadn't seen my wife and son, but no one was saying anything about leave so that was the second factor that prompted me to make a decision.

Next day the company's Marine Superintendent came aboard and Fergie was delegated to ask me if I was staying with the ship. I simply replied, "No, I'm signing off and I'll not be back". I packed my kit, signed off on the 21st March 1946 and crossed the Mersey by ferry for the last time.

That was it. My Certificate of Discharge from the Merchant Navy Service arrived a few days later. It was dated April 3rd 1946. There was no 'thank you', no gratuity and no demob suit, but a lot of pride and a host of memories remain.

I started off these memoirs by saying how lucky I had been to survive and I've repeated that statement more than once. The more I thought about these events and as I wrote them down, I became aware of how I had often been transferred from areas of conflict as they became more dangerous and sent elsewhere.

When on the 'Plate run' on the St. Merriel there was always the danger from roving surface raiders and submarines. Although one convoy I had been on was scattered, the U-boat menace off the approaches to Freetown did not really begin in earnest until after I transferred to the St. Clears.

It was whilst we were 'safely' frozen in at Bakaritza that the attacks on the Arctic convoys were organised with all their ferocity.

Whilst we were there, the number of attacks on the Atlantic con-voys soared. Returning home, we were saved by the fog and by the Germans concentrating their attack on poor PQ17.

After that, although I signed on with ships that were operating with the military in the Mediterranean, we were always in company and relatively well escorted in congenial weather.

I had been lucky—I'd survived. Many hadn't.

19

THE RECKONING

Saint Line losses:

The Saint line:

The South American Saint Line started the war with ten Saint boats, two of which survived. The St. Rosario, although bombed and damaged twice, survived and was sold in 1952. The other survivor was the St. Clears (!) which was sold in 1957. There was also the strange case of the St. Winifred, sold to the Italians in 1938 and torpedoed by a British submarine in 1941.

The Fate of the Saint Line Fleet

Ship	Her Fate	Date Lost
St. Winifred.	Sold to the Italians in 1938.	09.0 3.1941
	Torpedoed by a British submarine.	
St. Glen	Bombed and sunk.	06.09.1940
St. Elwyn	Torpedoed.	28.11.1940
St. Helena	Torpedoed.	12.04.1941
St. Lindsay	Lost without trace, probably torpedoed.	14.06.1941
St. Merriel	Bombed and sunk in Bone Harbour.	02.01.1943
St. Margaret	Torpedoed.	27.02.1943
St. Essylt	Torpedoed.	04.07.1943
St. Usk	Torpedoed.	20.09.1943
St. Clears	Survived.	
	Sold in 1951 and was lost in 'Typhoon Wanda' 01.09.1962.	
St. Rosario	Survived, although bombed and damaged twice, Sold in 1952.	

The following ships were also managed by the Saint Line:

Ship	Her Fate	Date Lost
Shakespeare	Torpedoed.	05.01.1941
Chaucer	Sunk by the Orion commerce raider.	29.07.1941
Ripley	Torpedoed.	12.12.1941
Orminster	Torpedoed.	25.08.1944
Charlton Hall	Survived and was sold in 1954.	

Other Companies:

There were many of these of course, but we in the Saint Line knew those listed below very well.

The Larinaga Line lost nine of the fleet of twelve ships that they had in 1939. Of the nineteen replacement Forts, Oceans and Empires that they managed, nine were lost.

By the end of the war the Harrison Line had lost twenty-nine of their fleet of forty-five.

The Hain Steamship Company (Hungry Hains), whose ship's names all began with Tre-, lost their entire fleet of twenty four ships.

The Houlder Line Ltd. of Liverpool lost 15 out of 22 ships, with one hundred and thirteen crew killed and ninety four captured.

The Blue Star Line (Vestey), who together with Houlders were the great pre- war meat importers from the Argentine, lost 29 out of 38 ships together with 646 personnel, including eleven Masters, forty seven Navigating Officers and eighty eight Engineers.

Table of Dates of Voyages.

Name of Ship	Shipping Company	Signed on	Signed off	Principal Destination and Events
St Merriel	Saint Line	14.01.1939	26.01.1939	The New Boy. North Sea Crossing to Antwerp
St Merriel	Saint Line	27.01.1939	14.05.1939	Learning the Ropes. First Voyage to South America
St Merriel	Saint Line	15.05.1939	28.08.1939	The East Coast of South America. Passengers on board.
St Merriel	Saint Line	29.08.1939	26.01.1940	Outbreak of War en route to South America. First Convoy.
St Merriel	Saint Line	27.01.1940	03.06.1940	The River Plate in South America. Man Overboard!
St Merriel	Saint Line	04.06.1940	18.12.1940	To South America and back around the north of Scotland.
St Merriel	Saint Line	19.12.1940	07.05.1941	Convoy will scatter—a long way home from Freetown.
St Merriel	Saint Line	08.05.1941	23.10.1941	South America Way. Shore leave with the Missionaries
St Clears	Saint Line	24.10.1941	13.07.1942	Arctic Convoy to the USSR. Frozen in at Archangel.
Forte a la Corne	MacGowan & Gross	12.11.1942	21.01.1943	Operation Torch—the Invasion of North Africa. Bone air raids.
Forte a la Corne	MacGowan & Gross	01.02.1943	30.03.1943	North Africa again. Torpedoed in the Med.
Fort Walsh	Larinaga Shipping Co.	01.06.1943	21.01.1944	The Invasions of Sicily and Italy. Salerno beach and Bari.
Ocean Gypsy	J & C Harrison	22.02.1944	04.03.1945	Tunisia and the Invasion of the South of France
Atheltarn	United Molasses	08.08.1945	21.03.1946	Bombay and Colombo. The End of Hostilities.

List of Abbreviations and Glossary

AB	Able Bodied Seaman.
Allotment	Part of wages 'allotted' elsewhere i.e. to one's wife
ATS	Auxiliary Territorial Service. The women's army.
AMC	Armed Merchant Cruiser.
AWOL	Absent without leave.
BA	Buenos Aires.
B & S	Bailey and Street Shipping Co. Cardiff.
Before the mast.	Figure of speech. As seaman rating in the foc'stle.
Blue Peter	International code flag 'P'. All aboard. Vessel is proceeding to sea.
Bosun	Boatswain. Petty Officer Seaman.
B o T	Board of Trade.
Bridge telegraph	Mechanical communication from bridge to engine room.
DEMS	Defensively Equipped Merchant Ships.
EMI	Electrical and Musical Industries.
FAM	Fast Aerial Mine.
Foc'stle	Forecastle. See drawing.
Gimbals	Pivoted device to ensure an object remains vertical or horizontal.
HF/DF	'Huff/duff'. Very high frequency direction finding.

Killick	Leading Seaman. RN.
Lower Deck	Figure of speech. As rating, not officer.
Min. of Ag.	Ministry of Agriculture.
MN	Merchant Navy.
MP	Military Police.
MS, MT, MV	Motor powered vessel.
MT	Motor Transport.
NCO	Non Commissioned Officer.
OS	Ordinary Seaman.
PAC	Parachute and Cable.
PO	Petty Officer.
RN	Royal Navy.
RNR	Royal Naval Reserve, usually merchantmen.
RNVR	Royal Naval Volunteer Reserve, from all walks of life.
SS	Steamship.
Sub	Sum of money paid from wages.
Subby	Naval Sub Lieutenant.
Tannoy	Loudspeaker system.
Ticket	Slang. Certificate of Competency.
UAC	United Africa Company.
WW1	1914—1918 World War.
WRNS	Women's Royal Naval Service.

EPILOGUE

Phillip Freshwater who was the Third Mate mentioned in the text sent this photograph of the Atheltarn to me in 2003. On a recent visit to Ludlow, mistakenly believing I had previously told him that I lived there, he 'found' me in the telephone directory. He and his wife walked in to see us—a reunion after fifty-seven years.

This photograph was taken in 1939—we don't know what port it was. Looking at it now, I have to say what a nice old fashioned looking tub the Atheltarn was with an attractive flare to the bows, a good shear and a nice 'tumblehome'—they don't make 'em like that any more!

n her peacetime colours of course: white superstructure,
d woodwork around the bridge and the letters UMC on the
or United Molasses Company Ltd. (the parent company of
nel Line), with plenty of black smoke coming out of it from
al fired boilers.

ote the change in paint colour below the bows which marks the
er line when fully loaded, follow it along to amidships and you
n see how little freeboard there was. I cannot distinguish any load
ine marks.

Below the bridge house there is a horizontal streak of light showing that it truly is a bridge with a passage beneath.

Right in the bows is the Mate with Chippy standing by the anchor windlass. This was routine procedure for entering and leaving
port. There are two figures on the bridge, probably the Old Man
and the Pilot or Third Mate.

She was built in Holland in 1917 and bought by the Athel Line
sometime in the 1920's. What she did in the war I don't know—I
don't remember there being any provision for armaments. Nor do I
know what happened to her after I left.